Dea

MW01518542

That you do —
Love,
Vivian Buxton

A Letter to My Grandchildren
and Other Correspondence

Reminiscences of a Holocaust Survivor

Bernard H. Burton

Dedicated to

Annie Riemer
Ruth Zadek
Hannah Zadek
Margot Silbermann
Günther Beiner
Arno Öttinger
Soldi Saphierstein
Harry Schmul
Gerd Wollstein
Ignatz and Selma Bäcker, their daughter Millie Bendix
and her husband
Max and Lina Kibak
Shlomo (Salo) Bäcker
Eugen Miloslawsky

Friends and family members murdered by the Nazis
between 1939 and 1944

May their memories be a blessing

Contents

Introduction

IN JANUARY 1929, a 30-year-old German journalist, Erich Maria Remarque, saw his first novel published under the title *Im Westen Nichts Neues*. A half a year later that novel, translated by A.W. Wheen, appeared in the USA as *All Quiet on the Western Front*. To this day, it is considered one of the foremost anti-war novels of the twentieth century. The novel speaks of the horrors of World War I, a time before I was born. It begins with a foreword, which I have taken from both the German and American editions.[1]

> *Dieses Buch soll weder eine Anklage noch ein Bekenntnis sein. Es soll nur den Versuch machen über eine Generation zu berichten, die vom Kriege zerstört wurde—auch wenn sie seinen Granaten entkam.*

> This book is to be neither an accusation nor a confession, and least of all an adventure, for death is not an adventure to those who stand face to face with it. It will try simply to tell of a generation of men who, even though they may have escaped shells, were destroyed by the war.[2]

---

[1] Erich Maria Remarque, *Im Westen Nichts Neues*. Berlin: Propyläen Verlag, 1929; and *All Quiet on the Western Front*. Boston: Little, Brown and Company, 1929.
[2] You will notice that the phrase "and least of all an adventure, for death is not an adventure to those who stand face to face with it" is an addition by the translator and does not appear in the original German text. I have not been able to find a clarification of this discrepancy. In the mid 1990s

My personal experiences as a Jewish boy growing up under the odious Nazi regime in Germany were "mild" in comparison with those of my late wife, some close relatives and friends. Most of them never lived to tell of the oppression they endured; they were killed! Yet, even my mild experiences, I believe, deserve to be told to my children and, perhaps more importantly, to my grandchildren.

For many years, I have written to editors of newspapers and corresponded directly with many people regarding different phases of the 4,481 days between January 30, 1933 (the day Adolf Hitler became Chancellor of Germany) and May 8, 1945 (the day Nazi Germany signed the unconditional surrender with the Allied Forces and effectively ceased to exist). These correspondences and the accompanying vignettes shed some light on my early youth—and what it meant for me to live under the Nazi regime. I have substantially expanded these materials by adding background information together with the beginning "Letter to my Grandchildren." Some details about my family and other events have also been added. Paraphrasing Remarque I can happily state I escaped the shells of that dark period in German and world history and luckily was not destroyed by it—although scars have remained to this day!

I dedicate this book to (1) Annie Riemer, née Adler, the mother-in-law I have never met; (2) eight of my twelve fellow graduates from the Jewish Middle High School in Berlin from which I graduated in March 1940: my first girlfriend Ruth Zadek and her twin sister Hannah, Margot Silbermann, Günther Beiner, Arno Öttinger, Soldi

---

I had contacted the late Tony Judt, at that time the director of the Remarque Institute of New York University. In a short answer he confirmed the difference but could not offer any explanation for it either. To me the shorter German original is much starker.

Saphierstein, Harry Schmul and Gerd Wollstein; and (3) my uncles and aunts Ignatz and Selma Bäcker, née Grätz (and their daughter Millie Bendix and husband), Max and Lina Kibak, née Bäcker and Shlomo (Salo) Bäcker, and my cousin Eugen Miloslawsky. Between 1939 and 1944 the Nazis killed these 17 wonderful people—all between the ages of about 18 and 65—whom I have mentioned in this paragraph. Their "crime" was the fact that they were Jewish.

I gratefully remember my uncle and aunt Ernst and Fanny Kleinmann, née Burstein. Without their foresight, material assistance and constant prodding I would not have survived. They were the only people I have ever met who correctly foresaw (before 1933) what was going to happen in Germany! They supported my parents and me financially from 1938 (when my father was dismissed from his job in Berlin) to 1945 when we finally arrived in the USA. They also paid all expenses in connection with our emigration from Germany to Cuba and to our final destination, the USA.

Lastly, I would like to thank all of you who are reading my reminiscences. Please keep in mind, however, that this is not a history primer. I have tried to be careful and to indicate the sources of any facts I have mentioned throughout the book. On the other hand any expressions of opinions are entirely my own. A reader may come to different conclusions using these same facts.

The Holocaust

THIS TERM REPRESENTS the state-sponsored, systematic persecution and later annihilation of European Jewry by Nazi Germany and its collaborators, between January 30, 1933 and May 8, 1945. It is estimated that six million Jews were murdered.

The word "holocaust" appeared first in the Holy Scriptures (I Samuel 7:9). In Hebrew, the word was *churban*, meaning an offering to God that is entirely burnt. Translated into Greek the word became *holokauston*, which in English turned into holocaust. While the word was occasionally used over the centuries, it only became common usage at the Second World Congress of Jewish Studies held in Jerusalem in July–August 1957. The word was then used when referring to the Nazi genocide. For more than 40 years, it has also been applied to mass slaughters of other peoples. Many scholars are now using the Hebrew word *shoah* (calamity). In my writing, however, I have used it in its original (1957) context.

1

A Letter To My Grandchildren

DEAREST Rachel, Nicole, Daniel, Jake and David:
I have always regretted the fact that I had never known my grandfathers, nor do I really know much about them. My maternal grandfather, Berl Bäcker, died before I was born (and I was named after him), and the other, Josef Burstein,[3] passed away when I was two years old, much too young to remember him. Now I am a grandfather myself, and while I am in good mental and physical health, I decided to write this letter to you.

I am going to cite just two incidents of my life that took place when I was 15 and 17 years old. I talk about them because they occurred as part of what is now called "the Holocaust." It is my sincere hope, as you grow older, that you study this period of man's inhumanity to Jews. By a twist of fate, my parents and I escaped almost certain death at the last minute. I also hope that by talking about what happened to me, I can put this period into human terms and show that in spite of everything that might have warned us to expect the worst, there were people (and my

---

[3] I was born Burstein, but chose to become a "Burton" as part of my naturalization as a U.S. citizen. I have discussed this further in the chapter "My Service in the U.S. Army."

father was among them) who simply could not fathom how human beings could or would behave toward each other!

The Arrest

ON SEPTEMBER 21, 1939 at around 7:00 in the morning, someone rang the doorbell at our modest one-bedroom apartment in the center of Berlin (Magazinstrasse 2). My mother was preparing breakfast for me, and shortly thereafter I was scheduled to leave for school. I was standing behind my mother when she opened the door. Two middle-aged Berlinese police officers were outside the door and told us they had come to arrest my father. No reason was given. This had happened at other times over the last several years to Jewish people we knew but it had never happened to us. Incidentally, the Nazis' arresting Jews without cause even before the war had begun dispels the notion that the Holocaust was a wartime measure.

The police officers waited in the living room while my mother went into the bedroom to inform my father. Just as my father finished getting dressed and came out of the bedroom, the doorbell rang again. Another police officer was outside; he had come to arrest me. I was a little more than 15 years old at that time.

My mother's face became ashen, and she argued that there must be a mistake—kids were not to be arrested[4]—to no avail. Now the third officer met with my father, and upon seeing him, addressed him with the familiar *Du*, inquiring whether he had attended a certain grammar school some 30-odd years earlier. That police officer and my father recognized each other as having been

---

[4] It was common knowledge among Jews that by order of the German secret police (Gestapo) of January 21, 1939 all Jewish prisoners below the age of 18 years who had been arrested in November 1938 were to be released. This order obviously did not help me.

in the same grammar school classes, but they had not seen each other in the intervening years.

The same officer then asked my mother whether she wanted to accompany us to the police precinct so she could again state her case with regard to my age. Under the then-existing circumstances that was all he could do for us, especially under the watchful eyes of his two colleagues. My parents, the three police officers and I walked to the police station[5] while our neighbors stared at us.

My father's school acquaintance talked briefly to the sergeant on duty and then turned to my mother, in effect encouraging her to speak. To my utter amazement, the following dialogue ensued.

Mother: "You have arrested my son. He is too young to be taken. He is only 15."

Police Sergeant: "When was he born?"

M: "On the seventh of April 1924."

PS: "Then he is over 15 years old."

M: "Yes."

PS: "I have been ordered to arrest male Jews over the age of 15."

M: "What is the reason for this arrest?"

PS: "I don't know. I am just following orders."

M: "Well, the day of reckoning will come!"

PS (after a long pause, looking at my mother): "You should not have married a Jew, and then you would not have had any problem today!"

All I could do during this short exchange was to stand in awe. From the onset of the Nazi regime, I had been brought up to "blend in," not to talk back, not to make any waves, to try to be as unobtrusive as possible. Now,

---

[5] The nearest police precinct was located next to our apartment building at Magazinstrasse 3–5. It had been built in the early twentieth century and has been recently classified as a historical monument. The police of the Land of Berlin presently use it as an administrative office.

here, that same woman who had taught me these "survival skills" suddenly became a lioness. She asked the authorities to provide evidence when arresting a person, as if we had been living in a democracy.

The sergeant, in his own way, must also have been surprised. Mutti, as I called her, did not achieve her goal to obtain my release. She did, however grudgingly, gain the respect of the police sergeant. Little did he know that my mother, a blue-eyed blonde-haired person, was born to an Orthodox Jewish family. However, in the parlance of Germany at that time, she did not "look Jewish." I have always wondered what might have happened if the police sergeant had thought that my mother was Jewish. I actually was afraid for her, expecting to witness her arrest because of her outspoken defense. To this day, I consider the few words she used a turning point in my own feelings about the regime. Her attempt filled me with hope and optimism for the future. (Incidentally, we never saw or heard from my father's school acquaintance again.)

After a tearful goodbye with my mother, my father and I were taken to a holding cell, which within the next few hours was filled with friends and acquaintances. Nobody had any idea why we had been arrested, nobody knew where we would be sent and all of us were apprehensive. We were not permitted to speak to each other, so eye contact and body language had to suffice.

Later we were put onto a police prison bus and left the precinct. The trip did not take too long, probably less than an hour. We were told to get off in front of the exhibition halls near the Berlin radio tower, in the western part of the city.[6] This area was familiar to me because I had

---

[6] In an amazingly forward-looking policy—at the height of the 1923 inflation—the Berlin city administration started an impressive modernization move. One result was the developing of Berlin's position as a conference and exhibition center, and the staging of the first

8

attended, until November 1938, the yearly radio, health and other exhibitions.[7]

At that moment, I did not know that the exhibition halls had been "converted" into a "DULAG," short for *Durchgangslager*, or transit camp. The entire conversion consisted of two changes. Several inches of straw had been put on the floors, and on top of a large staircase leading to Exhibition Hall Eight, where we had been placed, a machine gun had been set up to cover the entire hall. From here, those who were arrested were later sent to concentration camps or newly-established ghettos[8] in Nazi-occupied Poland.

At this makeshift transit camp we were turned over by the police to the SS.[9] A change of attitude was immediate. As a "punishment" for having arrived late (it

---

German Radio Exhibition in 1924. The exhibition halls were built for this occasion and set new international standards. See also Thomas Friedrich, *Berlin Between the Wars*. New York: The Vendome Press, 1991.

[7] A law, which became effective on December 6, 1938, prohibited Jews from attending theaters, movie houses, museums, and any public functions or sports arenas. This law is covered in greater detail in the chapter "My Middle Name Was Israel and Other Indignities."

[8] In context of the Holocaust, the term "ghetto" refers to certain urban areas in Nazi-occupied Poland and the Soviet Union, in which the Nazis forced Jews to live under crowded and miserable conditions. The goal was to keep Jews isolated and controlled while the Nazis determined what to do about the "Jewish Question." The word "ghetto" itself originally referred to the Jewish quarter in Venice, Italy in the early sixteenth century, where Venetian Jews were forced to live. The term then came to refer to any area where Jews were concentrated by force, and ultimately became a word used to refer generally to disadvantaged urban neighborhoods.

[9] Originally founded by Hitler in the mid 1920s with perhaps 200 men as his personal bodyguards, "SS" is an abbreviation for *Schutzstaffel*—Protection Squadron. The SS members wore black uniforms similar to those of Mussolini's Fascists. They were also made to swear a special oath of loyalty to Hitler personally. The SS grew in size and importance and eventually controlled the secret police, administered the concentration and extermination camps and even became an army outside the regular German Army, known as the *Waffen SS* (SS Forces).

was about 6:00 in the evening), we and the other Jewish prisoners who had come from all parts of Berlin were marched inside the hall towards a long wall, and facing it, were made to stand until midnight. Those who collapsed were not helped and the SS prohibited the prisoners from helping each other. Nobody had had anything to eat or drink since we were arrested.

Then we were told to stand in a different line if we had to urinate. (The SS did not quite use such civilized language.) The latrines had been previously erected in a courtyard within the exhibition hall compound. About 150 to 200 people were then marched to these latrines and from both sides the SS troopers suddenly and without any provocation used their rifle butts to beat the men who were now running towards the latrines in order to escape the beatings. My father and I were lucky not to have been hit but I remember seeing men with ripped clothing and bleeding legs and shoulders.

It was in that early morning hour of September 22, 1939 that I suddenly grew up. I was born and had always lived in Germany. Around my ninth birthday, the country had turned into a dictatorship and had enacted ever more stringent anti-Semitic laws. Therefore, I really had never known the concept of democracy or enjoyed freedom as you understand and I hope will cherish; but to some degree, this was my mental salvation. When you have never known freedom, living in a prison is easier to endure!

Until that morning, I had been an only child protected by loving parents, attending an exceptionally fine Jewish high school, one of the oldest in Germany; its roots went back to Moses Mendelssohn[10] in 1778. A former

---

[10] Moses Mendelssohn (1729–1786), a German Jewish philosopher of the Enlightenment and pioneer of the emancipation of Jews in

principal of that school wrote that the school had had to take the place for the losses in the world around it—and in fact the school had become an oasis of pleasure and calm. Within the school there was work, learning and a future while outside of the school there was stagnation, decay and the ever-trying and agonizing present.[11] On September 22, 1939 I became a part of that "present."

Every day the SS thought of different "games" to play with their Jewish prisoners. One night an Orthodox man with a long white beard was roused with kicks and rifle butts from the straw on which we were sleeping. He was photographed (rumor had it the pictures were taken for *Der Stürmer*)[12] and when he was returned a few hours later his beard had been shorn.

One day a man was thrown by an SS trooper against a plate glass door, which broke, in addition to injuring the poor soul. The entire group was then forced to pay 84 marks for the door. It was not a huge sum, but collecting the money became difficult because in many police precincts (not in ours) the police had confiscated any money carried by anyone arrested. Moreover, most of the

---

Germany, was a founder of the "Jewish Free School" in Berlin, which eventually became the Jewish Middle High School, which I attended.

[11] Heinemann Stern, *Warum hassen sie uns eigentlich?* (Why do they really hate us?) Düsseldorf, Germany: Droste Verlag, G.m.b.H., 1970.

[12] *Der Stürmer* was the worst anti-Semitic weekly printed in Nazi Germany. Its publisher, Julius Streicher, was among the few Nazi leaders condemned to death (and later hanged) following the Nuremberg trials after World War II. The paper used the slogan *Die Juden sind unser Unglück* (Jews are our misfortune). I had always been of the opinion that this slogan originated with the Nazis. To my great surprise, however, I discovered that Heinrich von Treitschke (1834–1896), a German nationalistic historian whose writings reflected his anti-Semitic and anti-British feelings, coined this *Schlachtruf* (battle cry), as he called it. On November 15, 1879, von Treitschke published an article, *Unsere Aussichten* (Our Prospects), discussing the then-current political situation in Bismarckian Germany. The text included the infamous phrase that became the standard motto of anti-Semitic agitation during the Nazi period: "Jews are our misfortune."

other people had just a few marks in their pockets; I had but pennies. Nevertheless, we were able to pay for the "malicious damage caused by a Jewish prisoner." And the beatings continued—but only at night!

There was one incident during my incarceration that might almost be called comical. Several times daily all men were ordered to stand in a quasi-military formation for roll call (*Appell*) to listen to whatever gibberish, insults or occasional instructions were being heaved upon us.

At times, some SS officers accompanied by their staff passed in review of the prisoners and would pick individuals at random in order to insult them. On one such review, an officer stopped in front of me and barked: "Are you a Jew?" "Yes, sir," I answered. Not satisfied, he continued: "Are you a full Jew?" (*Bist Du ein Volljude?* —a Nazi term, inquiring whether both of my parents were Jewish.) Again, I answered "Yes, sir." As the officer walked away, continuing his "inspection," I could hear him saying to his cohorts, "You can get fooled by him."

In between the "games" and the interminable roll calls, we were not permitted to roam around the exhibition hall but were forced to lie on the straw. Talking, or better said, whispering, was therefore limited to those who were closest to you. My father was on one side of me and to the other was a friend from school (Gerald Bocian) and his father next to him.

To the best of my recollection, there were only four boys in the group of prisoners. I was the second youngest. About three days after the arrest, while we were still in the same exhibition hall, in the same clothing, unwashed, the SS started to call prisoners by name. Groups of men were then taken away. I have no personal knowledge of what happened to them except for two people.

The youngest prisoner was an acquaintance from school by the name of Mandelkern. I only remember his last name. Taken away, he was sent to the infamous concentration camp Sachsenhausen where he survived for 11 months. He was then discharged, returned to his mother, re-arrested about a month later and "deported" to Poland. I never heard from him again.

Another man, an acquaintance of my parents', was deported to a ghetto in Lublin, Poland. I have seen one brief letter he mailed months later to his wife and children, then still living in Berlin. That was the last time anyone ever heard from him.

There was one other event during my incarceration which I will never forget. When I did not appear in school on September 22, my friend Irving Klothen and my girlfriend Ruth Zadek visited my apartment and heard from my mother what had happened. Upon their return visit the next day, having found out where my father and I were being kept, my mother handed them a paper bag with a loaf of bread and about six apples, which my friends took to the exhibition hall. They talked to one of the SS guards and requested that this precious bag be delivered to me. Miracles do happen sometimes! I actually received the bag intact, together with a handwritten note they had inserted expressing their friendship.

Yet, that was not the end of this remarkable story. My mother, who was always concerned about my table manners, had also put a knife into the bag. After all, in order to eat properly one must be able to slice the bread. When I saw the knife, I became worried. What do you do with a sharp kitchen knife after you have been jailed?

I approached one of the inside SS guards and explained what had happened. He was not interested and simply told me to throw the knife away (*Schmeiss es weg*). That was easier said than done. However, I noticed a rubbish bin. When nobody was looking, I pushed the knife into the garbage.

After five or six days, the number of prisoners remaining in the transit camp had become smaller. Finally, one late afternoon both my father's and my names were called and together with a group of perhaps 20 other people we were told to go home. "We do not need you!" To the best of my recollection, we were the only group to be released; we had been arrested "by mistake!" Naturally, we did not ask any questions and either walked home or took public transportation (those that still had any money left).

The next day I went back to school. I graduated on March 29, 1940, in probably one of the last graduation ceremonies of a Jewish high school in Nazi Germany.[13] Of the twelve graduating students (eight boys and four girls), one girl died in Berlin, probably unrelated to the Holocaust, after I had left Germany. The Nazis killed the remaining three girls and five of the boys. I have mentioned their names in the introduction to this book. One boy, Irving Klothen, emigrated with me. The other was Gerald Bocian. He had also been arrested and released with me from the transit camp. Later, he survived incarceration at the Theresienstadt concentration camp and arrived in the U.S. after the war. With the loss of Irving, who passed away on June 12, 2008, Jerry and I are the only survivors from that graduating class.

The Window Seat To Freedom

THE SHOCK OF the albeit short imprisonment finally propelled my father to accept the entreaties of his older sister who by then lived in the U.S. She had been trying

---

[13] The number of Jewish schools was gradually reduced on account of emigration and—starting in 1938—forceful expulsion. An order of June 20, 1942 (11 months after I had left Germany) required all Jewish schools to cease operating effective July 1, 1942. It also prohibited any further education for Jewish children.

since February 1933 (!) to persuade her brother and family to leave Germany, and had correctly predicted at that time that in the long run, nobody would be interested in the fate of the Jews in Germany. (Humphrey Bogart exclaimed in 1942 in the movie *Casablanca*, "It doesn't take much to see that the problems of three little people don't amount to a hill of beans in this crazy world.") While emigration was difficult for all Jews, it had become more so for us because Papa may have been too rigid in the early years of the Hitler regime regarding the countries he would consider for settlement. Soon it was literally too late, as one country after another closed its borders to the immigration of Jews. I have expanded on this topic in the chapter "Trying to Emigrate."

In early 1940, a window of escape opened. My aunt had obtained documents for our family to immigrate to the Dominican Republic, one of the few countries in the world still accepting Jewish refugees. At that late date, the choice of country did not matter anymore! We were scheduled to sail from Italy around the beginning of June. In May, however, the trip on the Italian liner was canceled, and Italy entered the war on Germany's side on June 10, 1940. Therefore, we continued to be stuck in Germany.

Soon it was late spring 1941; Germany had been at war for more than a year and a half and the situation of Jews in Germany had become still more precarious. Some German provinces were already *judenrein*, "cleansed of Jews." This term at that time implied that those provinces had been "cleaned" since the Jews had left, mostly by deportations to the German-occupied part of Poland. Those of us still in Berlin did not know of the existence of extermination camps, but we did hear that Jews from Germany were sent to ghettos in Poland. We also became aware that some Jews from Berlin itself were taken there.

Given the above-mentioned scenario, my parents and I were extremely fortunate that my aunt was able to arrange for transit visas to Cuba. There were no direct connections from Europe to the Dominican Republic, and so these visas (obtained at a substantial financial cost) were essential in allowing us to immigrate by way of a transatlantic crossing from Spain and a crossover in Cuba. In order to leave Germany proper we had to get special permission to travel, by rail, via German-occupied France to Spain.

Every one of these steps meant getting proper documents and transportation in advance, which took several months and would again have been impossible without the generous moral and financial support of my aunt. Remember also in those days we had no way of sending information or documents by telephone or electronically.[14]

Regardless of any documentation obtained, Jewish men were no longer permitted to emigrate if they were between 18 and 45 years old (i.e. if they were capable of serving in the armed forces of another country). My parents and I received the most important exit permit on July 7, 1941. On that day, I was seventeen years and three months old and my father forty-five years and five months—both of us within several months of deadlines that would have made it impossible to escape the clutches of the Nazis.

---

[14] The progression of anti-Jewish laws proclaimed by the Nazi government can be easily seen in the following simple compilation regarding the use of telephones. Starting on April 22, 1933 the use of "Jewish" names for spelling, while dictating a telegram by telephone, was prohibited. As of July 13, 1936 blind Jewish war veterans (i.e. Jews who had lost their eyesight while fighting for Germany in World War I) no longer had a right to reduced telephone rates. Effective July 29, 1940 Jews were prohibited from subscribing to telephone service. From December 12, 1941 on, Jews were also prohibited from using public telephones.

By then the visas for entry to the Dominican Republic were more than one year old, and my father and I decided one day to visit the consulate in Berlin. An employee advised us that the visas in our passports had indeed expired and new ones, if they were to be granted at all, would take several months to be obtained. As we left the consulate, and I remember that moment to this day, my father admonished me not to mention to anyone, including my mother, what we had just been told.

It was on the basis of these expired visas for the final destination—*which to our life-saving luck no authority ever questioned*—that all the above documents and permits were added to our passports.

The last and final step was now the purchase of railroad tickets from Berlin to the Spanish border. This might seem easy. You would think that all that was necessary was to go to a travel bureau to buy the tickets. In reality, it was much harder since the users of these tickets were Jews trying to leave wartime Nazi Germany.

In order to speed up emigration of Jews from Germany a central office had been established on January 24, 1939 within the Ministry of Interior. This office was placed under the overall supervision of the Security Police. As part of the Jewish Community Council in Berlin, a separate office, reporting indirectly to the above-mentioned one, was designated by the Nazis to coordinate the distribution of railroad tickets.

Those relatively few Jews who were lucky enough to have obtained all the other paraphernalia to emigrate had to report on a daily basis to that office. Every day an official of the German railroad would tell the Jewish coordinator how many people would be accommodated that *same* evening on a train leaving for German-occupied France.

I recollect that there was at least one train leaving Berlin daily for Paris and beyond, mostly for soldiers returning to their garrisons in France. One railroad car was added on occasion to that train, permitting Jews to leave. As far as I know these railroad tickets had to be paid for in hard currency by relatives or refugee organizations abroad, or at exorbitantly high prices for the few people that still had assets in Germany. Germany also obtained another bonus. Since the departure date was only set on the same day, apartments with furniture and whatever other assets remained were then confiscated for the "welfare" of the Reich. The (Jewish) coordinator picked the number of people he had been allotted from among those in the waiting group based on priority, i.e. depending upon when the ships from Spain or Portugal (the neutral countries) were scheduled to sail.

Some days there was no Jewish wagon so nobody could emigrate, perhaps because the regular train was crowded or some other matter; no reason was ever given. The number of available seats also varied.

Finally, in the middle of July 1941, my father was handed three tickets for that evening's train. He looked at the tickets and wondered aloud whether at least one of them was a window seat. The coordinator was probably (and rightly) annoyed at the question and curtly said there were no more window seats available, whereupon my father returned the tickets to him, explaining that he would not leave without at least one window seat!

The people next in line received the three tickets and my father came home that afternoon telling my mother that we would have to wait with our emigration for one more day, since we were now at the top of the list.

I have never found out why my father reacted that way. More than 20 years later (and Papa immediately remembered what I was referring to) I asked him why he had been so insistent about a window seat. He reacted to my question with a nervous laugh but did not go any further. I felt that he did not want to delve into the circumstances surrounding that difficult time (and his obvious almost fatal mistake), and I never again brought this matter up with him. Only one explanation makes sense to me. Your great-grandfather was a very simple man, born and bred in Berlin, did not know at that time any language other than German, and at age 45 had never in his life been more than perhaps 100 miles away from that city. I believe he suddenly panicked when he realized that he was about to leave Germany.

The next day there was no Jewish wagon at all, nor on the following day, and immediately rumors circulated that emigration for Jews was being terminated altogether. Luckily, about three days later emigration was resumed, and we left Berlin in a sealed wagon "for Jews only," with two window seats. Each traveler was permitted to take along one suitcase with personal belongings and the U.S. dollar equivalent of ten marks—for the three of us that amounted to a total of $11.65. (In 2011 dollars that would have amounted to about $178.) My parents were also "allowed" to wear their gold wedding rings but no other pieces of jewelry. One steel-encased wristwatch per person was also permitted to be taken along.

We boarded the train in the early evening of July 18, 1941 with perhaps 25 other lucky emigrants. All window shades were drawn, a wartime blackout requirement; but the next morning the Nazi conductor prohibited us to raise the shades. As usual no reason was given.

Our train went west to France and eventually to Spain. I believe we arrived in Paris on July 19, 1941 where our wagon stayed overnight. The following morning it was hitched to another train for the Spanish border. Only then were we permitted to look out of the windows—and we were on our way to freedom. Before that last step, however, we had to submit to one final indignity. At the Hendaye railroad station, our papers were minutely examined by German *Grenzpolizei* (border police) and by French customs officials working under the watchful eyes of their German masters. Both groups were fear-inspiring. The one suitcase we each carried was inspected in detail. Not a single word was exchanged. Yet, we knew that the border police literally had the power to give us life or death—by allowing us to proceed or by turning us back.

Eventually we received permission to cross, by foot, a small wooden bridge from German-occupied Hendaye[15] in France to Irún, Spain. We started to breathe again. The date was July 21, 1941.

We did not know it at that time, but we had beaten the total emigration ban for Jews from Germany by 98 days! An edict issued on October 27, 1941 by the *Reichssicherheitshauptamt* (Chief Security Office of the Reich) stated in part "... for the duration of the war and without exception the emigration of Jews is prohibited." (*Die Auswanderung von Juden ist ausnahmslos für die Dauer des Krieges verboten.*) The same edict then declared, "in lieu of emigration [of Jews] and in accordance with prior approval by the Führer [Hitler] the solution now lies in their evacuation to the East." This was Nazi shorthand for the forced transfer of Jews to German-occupied Poland and their eventual annihilation. Nine days

---

[15] One of the important but lesser-known turning points of World War II had taken place in Hendaye about a year before our border crossing. Hitler and Francisco Franco, the Spanish dictator whom Hitler had helped to win the Spanish Civil War, had met in Hendaye. Fortunately for all of us, Hitler had been unsuccessful in trying to entice Franco to enter the war on the side of the Axis powers, even though he had "promised" him Gibraltar. Had Franco accepted that proposal, it would have eliminated the last escape route for my parents and me. More importantly, however, it might have also lengthened World War II, as with Spain's help Germany would have been able to seal off the Mediterranean.

prior to the issuing of this order, and exactly three months after our departure from the same city (but from a different railroad station), on October 18, 1941, the first "organized" deportation of Jews from Berlin took place. On that day 1,089 people were sent east to the Litzmannstadt (Lodz) ghetto in occupied Poland. This ghetto eventually became the second largest after Warsaw. No one I knew was included in that deportation, but the short time that had elapsed since our departure highlights again how close we might have come to being deported ourselves.

Some Final Thoughts

AS YOU HAVE read this letter, the question might have occurred to you how one can recall all these details, including dates and times of day, almost 70 years later. Here I have to mention an unusual event.

My very good friend Harry (Hermann) Pomeranz, whom I had met in school when I was ten years old, had left Germany with his parents in December 1938 and gone to Uruguay. From that time on we corresponded with each other, naturally in a guarded fashion since letters were subject to German censorship—officially since September 1939, but unofficially much earlier.

After I had left Germany and upon his urging, I completed a ten-page single-spaced typed letter detailing my experiences in Germany after his emigration. Harry immigrated later to the USA. He died, unfortunately, in November 1980 at the age of 56. Some time later Lottie, his widow, found my long letter among his papers and returned it to me. As I reread my almost contemporaneous notes of my last years in Germany, many additional details, long forgotten, as if by miracle, came to mind. I do not think that I would have been able to write this current letter to you without relying, in part, on my earlier one kept by Harry for 39 years.[16]

Another point bears also to be mentioned. You must have noted that I have been very factual in describing the events. I made only minor references to the emotional side of my story. (Your mothers will tell you that I can be very emotional!) I have not told you how I felt in the transit camp or when I said goodbye to my mother, nor did I say anything about what went on in my mind when my father unnecessarily delayed our emigration—and I simply knew he had been wrong.

I did not do this deliberately. As much as I search my memory, I have no recollection of how I felt at those times. One thing I do know is that I have always been an optimist. At no time, and as afraid as I might have been, did I ever think I would not survive. However, exactly what went on in my mind I just cannot recall.

There is one thing I can point to that is a result of the fear I experienced when I was arrested. The late Claude Bourdet, a French Resistance leader and post-World War II editor, was incarcerated in a Nazi concentration camp and briefly imprisoned years later by the French for his outspoken views on the French campaign against Algerian independence. Bourdet wrote in his first post-prison editorial: "When somebody rings your bell at 6 AM and it is the milkman, you are living in a democracy."[17]

That quote brought to mind my life-long struggle—which I have never previously discussed—to open the front door when the bell sounded. If anything stuck with me from my arrest at age 15, it was this phobia against opening the front door, no matter where I lived. Only in the last ten

---

[16] I have donated the original letter to the Jewish Museum in Berlin. Harry's son Ken, a friend and preeminent historian, has done me the honor of reviewing this book. His comments appear on the back cover.

[17] Quoted in an obituary for Claude Bourdet written by Lawrence Van Gelder in *The New York Times*, March 22, 1996.

or fifteen years or so have I recovered from this traumatic experience.

During the early war years we were praying for the British to bomb Berlin (the USA was still a neutral country). When the bombers did come, we were naturally afraid for our lives. Many nights I sat with my parents and neighbors on the Jewish side of the apartment building's air-raid shelter[18]—and as afraid as I was, I usually took along my English or Spanish shorthand practice books. These studies represented the future, and as an optimist, even while "under fire" I expected to be part of that future. As I wrote before, the day after my release from the transit camp I went back to school, not once thinking that I should take a respite. Life must go on!

Epilogue

IN DECEMBER 1945, a little more than four years after my emigration (and eight months after my arrival in this country) I was drafted into the U.S. Army, and in November 1947 I was back in Berlin. I arrived by train, as an American soldier serving in Military Intelligence; and as I walked among the ruins of the exhibition halls I finally

---

[18] The chief of police of the city of Berlin, Wolf-Heinrich Graf von Helldorf,* issued an order, dated September 21, 1940, requiring that in apartment houses occupied by Jews and other tenants, separate air-raid shelters were to be installed for Jews in order to keep them apart from the other renters. This became probably one of the few anti-Jewish orders in Germany that was not followed completely—not because of a lack of will, but because in most cases, it was logistically not feasible to erect separate shelters. In our apartment house, the solution was for all Jewish tenants to sit in one corner of the shelter and neither mix with nor talk to the other tenants.

* Graf von Helldorf had been an early member of the Nazi party who was appointed Berlin's chief of police (*Polizeipräsident*) in 1935, two years after the Nazis came to power. Years later, he became closely involved in the attempt to assassinate Hitler on July 20, 1944 and was executed as a "traitor" on August 15, 1944.

fully realized I was a free man!

I spoke to several people who worked in the neighborhood of these ruins, and some volunteered they had been there for the entire duration of the war—but nobody claimed to remember the existence of any transit camp or ever having seen any prisoners in the area.

I wish you a good life in a peaceful twenty-first century, blessed with health and freedom. Strive to be good citizens and fight against oppression and anti-Semitism. Respect your parents. Always remember that my background is also your background!

My deep love and affection will always be with you.

—Your Grandpa.

Below and on following page:
My German Passport for Foreigners, issued August 25, 1939
(Original donated to the Jewish Museum in Berlin)

GELTUNGSBEREICH / GELTUNGSDAUER
VALIDITÉ DU PASSEPORT

Der Paß gilt für *In- und Ausland*
Le passeport est valable pour

Der Paß wird ungültig mit Ablauf des
Le passeport expire le
25. August 1940

falls er nicht verlängert wird.
à moins de renouvellement.

Die Rückkehr nach Deutschland wird während der Geltungsdauer des Passes gestattet*).
Le retour en Allemagne est autorisé durant la validité du présent passeport*).

Es wird hiermit bescheinigt, daß der Inhaber die durch das
Lichtbild dargestellte Person ist und die darunter befindliche
Unterschrift eigenhändig vollzogen hat.
Le soussigné certifie, que la photographie et la signature apposées ci-
contre sont bien celles du porteur.

Berlin, den **25. Aug. 1939** den

Der Polizeipräsident in Berlin
Im Auftrage:

Unterschrift / Signature

*) Der Inhaber unterliegt jedoch dem Sichtvermerkzwang.
Toutefois le porteur est tenu à se procurer le visa d'entrée.

4

VERLÄNGERUNGEN
RENOUVELLEMENTS

1.
Verlängert bis *25. August 1941* einschließlich
Renouvelé jusqu'
den *23. 8. 1940*
Polizeipräsident in Berlin
Im Auftrage:
Unterschrift / Signature

2.
Verlängert bis *7. Juli 1942* einschließlich
-7. Juli 1941,
Polizeipräsident in Berlin
Im Auftrage: / Signature

3.
Verlängert bis _____ einschließlich
Renouvelé jusqu'

, den
le
Behörde / Autorité

Wappen-
stempel

Unterschrift / Signature

5

26

Below and on following page:

1. The expired visa to immigrate to the Dominican Republic, dated March 21, 1940. No German or other authorities ever realized that the visa had expired by the time it was used 16 months later.

2. Transit Visa to Cuba

3. Permission to leave Germany. The stamps on the upper right corner, bearing the numbers "5" and "3," show that an administrative fee of eight marks was collected at the time of departure. The Nazis were sure to "squeeze" money from Jewish émigrés until the last possible moment.

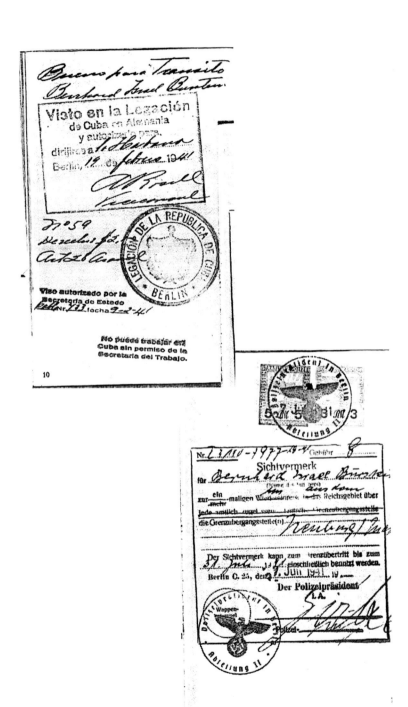

Visto en la Legación
de Cuba en Alemania
y autorizado para
dirigirse a *la Habana*
Berlín, *12* de *febrero* 1941

Nº 59

Visto autorizado por la
Secretaría de Estado
Berlín Nr. 793 fecha 9-2-41

No puede trabajar en
Cuba sin permiso de la
Secretaría del Trabajo.

10

Nr.
Gebühr

Sichtvermerk

für

ein
zur- maligen Wiedereinreise in das Reichsgebiet über
mehr
jede amtlich zugelassene deutsche Grenzübergangsstelle
die Grenzübergangsstelle(n)

Der Sichtvermerk kann zum Grenzübertritt bis zum
einschließlich benutzt werden.

Berlin C. 25, den

Der Polizeipräsident
I.A.

Wappen-
stempel

Polizei-

28

Top to bottom:
1. Stamp of the German Border Police upon leaving German-controlled Hendaye RR Station on July 21, 1941
2. Spanish Transit Visa, for one-time use, to pass through Spain to Cádiz, the original port of embarkation

Top to bottom:

1. Notation by the Dresdner Bank that I received the equivalent of ten marks in American currency

2. Spanish customs stamps showing entry into Spain with $3.35 and exit with the same amount

The Shipment To Switzerland

THE HIGHEST-RANKING Jewish academic institution in Berlin was the *Hochschule für die Wissenschaft des Judentums* (College for the Scientific Study of Judaism). This university-level school founded on May 6, 1872, was located in the "Barns' Quarter" (*Das Scheunenviertel*). I have discussed that section of Berlin in more detail in the chapter "Expiration Dates: September 12 and 30, 1941." At the time Hitler came to power the college had a library of about 40,000 books and manuscripts. I have mentioned these details to give the reader a better understanding of the discussion to follow.

An article under the heading "Ohio Professor Says He Was Smuggler of Hebrew Books" appeared in *The New York Times* on August 16, 1984. It concerned a former German Jew, then an 82-year-old emeritus professor at Hebrew Union College in Cincinnati, who said that he had foiled the Gestapo in Berlin around 1940 and smuggled to the U.S. 59 rare Hebrew books and manuscripts. The article explained the packing of these books at the professor's home, shortly before he immigrated to the USA.

The main reason for the article was obviously not the packing of the books (to which I shall return), but how the professor had gotten these books in the first place and what he now intended to do with them.

Dr. Alexander Guttmann was one of the last professors of the college to leave Germany in 1940. At that time, it was clear to the remaining academicians that the days of the college were numbered and that the library was in danger of being destroyed by the Nazis.[19] Dr. Guttmann offered to "illegally" take out some of the most valuable books and manuscripts. If he had been caught, I am certain, he would not have been able to emigrate and surely would have been sent to a concentration camp.

The institute's chairperson, according to Guttmann, stated "because of the enormous risk [taken by Guttmann], any such books ... that [Guttmann] did remove and thereby save from the Nazis would belong to him." As it happened, Dr. Guttmann achieved the almost impossible goal of smuggling the books out of wartime Nazi Germany. In 1984, 44 years later and in need of money, he attempted to sell the books and manuscripts at an auction in New York. (The Judaica Conservancy Foundation, a joint undertaking of Jewish colleges and universities in the U.S., London and Jerusalem, eventually obtained the books and manuscripts.)

According to the *Times* article Dr. Guttmann gave the Gestapo a false list of books that were packed. Since the packing was not completed in one day, the door to the room in his apartment where the packing was done was sealed. That night, Dr. Guttmann claimed, he entered the sealed room through an unlocked terrace door and replaced the ordinary books and manuscripts with those

---

[19] The College was officially closed and all its assets confiscated by the Gestapo on July 19, 1942. The remaining books and manuscripts were sent to Offenbach to be used after the war as part of a (Nazi) Library of the New Germany. Only a small part was ever recovered and is now in possession of the Leo Baeck College in London.

from the College.

The description of the packing of the professor's books brought back memories I had completely forgotten. As strange as it may seem in retrospect, with the war going on and all the other problems that had befallen Jews in Germany and the then German-occupied countries, it was still possible for Jews leaving Berlin to have some personal items packed—at their homes—under the supervision of a German customs official, and then shipped abroad by railroad. "Abroad" at this late date more often than not meant Switzerland. I do not know whether this was also possible from other places in Germany.

My father arranged for such a shipment to be readied. A packer from a local shipping company together with a customs official appeared at our apartment in June 1941 and in a few days packed and sealed two suitcases, four wooden crates and one large laundry bag, weighing a total of 662 kilograms (1,456 pounds). The customs official minutely inspected every item, mostly clothing and household articles; hence the reason the packing took so long. However, the official did not know that the packer had been "paid off" beforehand, and two new cameras (a Leica and a Contax) and about $100 in U.S. currency were also put into the suitcases.

I had several books I wanted to include in the shipment. I do remember a prayer book given to me at my Bar Mitzvah, some English and Spanish dictionaries and a few German novels. The customs man objected to the inclusion of these books without a special approval from the *Reichsministerium für Volksaufklärung und Propaganda* (Reich Ministry for People's Enlightenment and Propaganda). This ministry was under the leadership of the infamous Dr. Joseph Goebbels.[20]

---

[20] Goebbels and his wife committed suicide (after having poisoned their

The customs official suggested that I take a list of these books to the Ministry and request an approval for export. Once I had obtained such an approval, he would have no objection to their inclusion in the shipment. He even gave me directions to the Ministry.

With the list of books in hand, I left for the Ministry. This was a completely crazy mission given the time and circumstances. What happened there was later printed in my letter to the editor of *The New York Times* on August 31, 1984.

In writing this letter to the editor, I made two minor mistakes. My parents and I received permission to leave Germany in 1941, not 1940 as stated. Consequently, the visit to the Ministry of Propaganda had occurred in late spring of 1941.

I am also reprinting a letter I subsequently received from a *New York Times* correspondent, Henry Kamm. That letter mentioned that his box—also sent to Switzerland—was lost because his family could not afford to pay for the later shipment to America. The same sad ending happened to the few items (including the cameras and the money) that my family was able to ship to Switzerland. We never saw any of them again.

---

six children) on May 1, 1945 in front of Hitler's bunker in Berlin, one day before Berlin surrendered to Soviet troops.

My Letter to the Editor of *The New York Times*

A Jewish Boy and His Books in Nazi Germany

To the Editor:

Your Aug. 16 news article about the Ohio professor who smuggled rare books out of Nazi Germany reminded me of one of the few pleasant moments I had as a Jewish boy in wartime Germany.

In 1940, my parents and I received permission to leave Germany. In accordance with Nazi regulations, a customs official came to our house to supervise the packing and to seal those few belongings we were permitted to take along.

There were about 20 books which I wanted to pack. Among them were a prayer book I had received at my bar mitzvah, an English and Spanish grammar, some dictionaries and some German novels — nothing of great value and certainly in no way to be compared to the books Dr. Guttmann attempted to take out the same year.

The customs official, however, refused to allow these books to be packed since we had not requested prior permission from the Propaganda Ministry, which had jurisdiction over exports of "cultural material" (not the Gestapo, as stated in your article). My parents immediately decided not to take the books along. After all, who in his right mind would want to get involved with yet another Nazi official?

For some unknown reason, the customs official then turned to me and told me that if I were to type a list of the books, including publishers' names and dates, I could still go to the Ministry of Propaganda, apply for an export permit and with luck get one before we were to leave.

So in the spring of 1940, a 16-year-old Jewish boy went to Dr. Goebbels's ministry to request an export permit for his prize possession.

As luck would have it, I found the right department and talked to a young woman (she could not have been much older than I). Our eyes met for just a fleeting moment. I liked her, and I instinctively felt that the feeling was mutual.

I explained my request to her. Almost apologetically, she answered that she could not get me the required permit that day but would try to have it ready the following day, and I was to pick it up. She kept her promise, and the books were packed.

BERNARD H. BURTON
Manhasset Hills, L.I., Aug. 23, 1984

Letter from Henry Kamm
(text also appears on page 186)

The New York Times

ROME BUREAU

CORSO VITTORIO EMANUELE II, 154

TEL. 654-8293 - 659-889

September 11, 1984

Dear Mr. Burton,

Your letter to my editor stirred memories, still vaguely melanchonic. The customs man who came to my house, a year later, allowed us to pack our books, each listed like yours, without Propaganda Ministry approval. But, because the war had progressed by 1941, our few belongings got no further than Switzerland. We could not afford their shipment to America. I wonder who's reading them now.

As I write this, I am once again surrounded by packers, the nth time. Tomorrow I shall be leaving for Greece.

Forgive this letter of reminiscence from a stranger, but yours stirred and brought back to the forefront of the mind images long forgotten.

Yours sincerely,

Henry Kamm

36

3

The Beginning Air War Over Germany

FROM APRIL 1930 to 1934, I attended an elementary school in Berlin. According to the then-existing Prussian school system, a decision had to be made for a child approaching his/her tenth birthday regarding the continuation of schooling beyond those first four years. As far as I remember, there were three ways to continue the school process. The first one was to stay in the elementary school and to graduate at age 14. The second possibility was to transfer to an Intermediate High School (*Mittelschule*) with graduation at age 16, and the last was to enter a "Gymnasium" with graduation at age 18, which would then also allow the student to enter a university.

While parents may have desired the higher education for their children, to the best of my recollection acceptance was not automatic. High schools probably had their own admissions standards. My parents opted for the Jewish *Mittelschule*. This particular school had a very high academic rating, but more importantly, tuition at Berlin's only Jewish Gymnasium was financially out of their reach.

The principal of my elementary school had summoned my mother as early as the spring of 1933 and suggested that she transfer me to a Jewish school because life for Jewish students in the public school system would, in his words, become "impossible." The law prohibiting Jewish children from attending public schools took effect "only" on November 15, 1938. Yet, Dr. Lüdtke's very early warning to have me leave the public school system in April 1934, at the end of the school year, was of greatest help to my education and my mental well-being while still living in Nazi Germany—and I am most grateful to him.[21]

As part of the admissions procedure to the Jewish school, I had to submit my school grades and write an *Aufsatz* (essay). The same Dr. Lüdtke suggested that I write about our school's recent trip to an air raid shelter.

According to Nazi press reports of June 23, 1933, Allied airplanes of an unknown type were flying over Germany distributing anti-German leaflets. This was a deliberate false statement against the Versailles peace treaty, intended to highlight the fact that Germany was without anti-aircraft weapons. The reports ended with a warning that the next time the same planes might drop bombs instead of leaflets. I cannot recall whether I actually believed the propaganda. I possibly did, and my parents—if they believed otherwise—might have been too scared to say so. This is a very simple example, early on during the Hitler regime, of Dr. Goebbels's propaganda machine and the terrible pressure exercised by the suppression of freedom of expression. In some areas of Berlin, model air-raid shelters were built (more than five years before the beginning of the war!). The "inauguration" of the first such air raid shelter took place in October 1933. Schoolchildren and other groups were taken to these shelters to become acquainted with them. My elementary school was no

---

[21] A few months later Dr. Lüdtke lost his job as principal of the school and was transferred to another school (as a teacher) because of his pre-Hitler activities in the Social Democratic Party. (In German parlance at that time, he was *strafversetzt*—transferred as a punishment, and reduced in rank).

exception. (My essay was accepted.)

In view of the later events that the Jews in Germany had to endure, the following seems almost macabre. In the latter part of 1937, the Government, as part of its continuing air raid precautions, began to issue gas masks to the general population. This contraption, called *Volksgasmaske*, or people's gas mask, was also available to Jews. An office within Berlin's Jewish Community performed the distribution with the approval of the Air Ministry (*Reichsluftfahrtsministerium*).[22] I distinctly recall having been trained to use such a mask.

For about the first ten days at the beginning of the war in September 1939 all schools in Berlin were closed. This, of course, included the Jewish schools. However, the Civil Defense Authorities decreed that all public buildings be manned on a 24-hour basis in order to have personnel available to assist in case of air raids. Consequently, the principal of our school required the boys in the senior class (that included me) to stay at the school during the night. We slept on mats in the gym. In the morning, some of the girls from our class would join us and prepare hot drinks and sandwiches. Those days of "air-raid duty" were quite enjoyable. However, as these reminiscences show, the "good times" came to an early ending.

The first bombs fell on Berlin during the night of August 25 to 26, 1940 when a few British bombers managed to reach the city. They did not accomplish much. Three days later the next air raid was much more intense. The Germans claimed a toll of 12 people killed and 28 injured.

On November 6, 1941, or about three and a half months after I had left Germany, I gave my impressions

---

[22] Herbert Freeden. *Die jüdische Presse im Dritten Reich* (The Jewish Press in the Third Reich). Frankfurt/M: Jüdischer Verlag bei Athenäum, 1987, p. 120.

about the "real" air war to my friend Harry Pomeranz. Following is a verbatim translation of the original portion written in German:

> The importance of the Royal Air Force bombing attacks on Berlin was rather negligible. It is true that some houses were destroyed, quite a few in fact. Nevertheless, both Germany and England have to realize that you cannot achieve complete victory with air power alone. Besides, you cannot destroy the entire war industry of a country like Germany.
>
> You may be interested to hear that a house across the street from ours was bombed. The RAF had used high explosive bombs and it felt as if our apartment building was going to collapse. At that moment, no one asked who was a Jew and who was Aryan. All of us in the air-raid shelter jumped up and ran towards the emergency exits. Women started to scream and children were crying. When the all clear was given, the emergency services were already trying to clear the rubble in order to extricate the dead. Unfortunately, two people, acquaintances of my mother's and anti-Nazis, were killed. While I welcomed every attack by the RAF I was always shaking all over when it came.

Let me emphasize that these notes were based upon my experiences through July 1941 and were written in Cuba the following November. At that time, I had not yet heard of the destruction, on April 26, 1937, of the city of Guérnica in Spain by the German "Legion Condor" which assisted General Franco in overthrowing the Spanish government. That bombing attack is now considered to have been the first German "experiment" in the "modern" method of air raids. I certainly did not imagine either the intensity or the magnitude of future air raids during the 1942 to 1945 period (while I was safely in Cuba). Yet, my "strategic" hunch, as a 17-year-old boy, that air power alone would not be sufficient to defeat Germany proved to be correct. Air raids certainly weakened the German war machine and to some degree its morale, but it took armies of foot soldiers and tanks occupying every inch of German soil to bring about the downfall of the Nazi regime.

4

Expiration Dates:
September 12 and 30, 1941

BERLIN'S BIGGEST BARGAIN" was the title of an article by Karl E. Meyer that appeared on the editorial page of *The New York Times* on December 19, 1994.

Mr. Meyer marveled at Berlin's well-functioning public transit system, in his opinion "one of the best urban transport bargains in the world." He described the system as it existed in 1994. Yet, the Berlin I remembered from the early 1930s to 1941 always had an excellent combination of subway, bus, streetcar and metropolitan railway lines, all of which I had used repeatedly. (My parents never owned a car.)

In a letter to Mr. Meyer following the publication of his article, I stated:

> I have read with great interest your article in today's *New York Times* about "Berlin's Biggest Bargain" and agree wholeheartedly with you. ... An ex-Berliner, who was extremely lucky to escape the Nazis as a seventeen year-old in July 1941, I have fond memories of Berlin's transit system.
>
> ... At a time when the first transports of Jews being shipped to the East were already underway, the Berlin Transit System was still

issuing passes to Jewish schoolchildren allowing them to use their facilities at a reduced rate. I am enclosing a copy of my own pass. In accordance with the existing racial laws, I signed my middle name "Israel" to denote that I was Jewish.[23]

At the end of this chapter, I have shown both sides of the pass referred to above. The last stamped entry on the reverse side "30.9.1941" (September 30, 1941) was the expiration date. The passes were issued for six months at a time. Laws governing their issuance predated the Nazis.

On August 30, 1935, the Nazi regime published an order prohibiting local authorities to discriminate against the use of public transportation by Jews, stating that only "nation-wide" anti-Jewish laws can handle such matters. Following up on this order, Jews were prohibited, as of December 28, 1938, from using dining cars on the German railroad system. Again, however, the use of public transportation was specifically "allowed." ("Jews are not to be prohibited from using public transportation."—*Die Benutzung der öffentlichen Verkehrsmittel ist Juden nicht zu verbieten*.) A further order of July 2, 1939 stated that no *new* requests for school passes for Jewish students by Jewish schools would be granted. Since I had such a pass for many years, it was not cancelled.

The September 30 expiration of my own student pass brought to mind another piece of governmental paper with an expiration date of September 12, 1941. To discuss the latter date I must digress.

My paternal grandfather had fled the recurring pogroms[24] in Russia around 1894 and decided to take his

---

[23] For a detailed discussion of this degrading law, see the chapter entitled "My Middle Name was Israel and Other Indignities."

[24] "Pogrom," a Russian word for "desolation," eventually took on the meaning for the planned killing of helpless Jews and the destruction of

family to the USA, in effect following hundreds of thousands of other immigrants. The twist here is the fact that in search of the freedom and better life he so craved for himself and his family, he got no further than Berlin, Germany. There were large waves of Russian Jews who passed through Germany on their way to America. As early as 1882 and again in 1891, Jews already living in Germany formed assistance organizations for their co-religionists from Russia. The latter group was called *Deutsches Central-Comité für die russischen Juden in Berlin* (German Central Committee for the Russian Jews in Berlin).

On his way to America through Germany, my grandfather met compatriots from his hometown. They convinced him to stay in Berlin and found an apartment for him in one of the poorest sections of the city, substantially populated by Jews from Eastern Europe. On a smaller scale, this was Berlin's equivalent to New York's "Lower East Side" at the turn of the twentieth century.

He settled in an area called *Das Scheunenviertel* (Barns Quarter). The name of this part of the city goes back to 1672. Friedrich Wilhelm, the Grand Elector, had signed an edict giving Berlin new fire regulations. One of the rules covered the warehousing of grain and other agricultural products. They had to be stored "outside" the city. Basing his order on the above edict, a later commandant of the city of Berlin (Hans Christoph Friedrich Graf von Hacke) ordered the construction of 27 barns. Long after the barns were gone, the area was still considered unsuitable for the average burgher of Berlin.[25]

---

their property, either approved or led by the Tsarist Russian government.

[25] A square within easy walking distance from the Scheunenviertel to this day carries the name "Hackescher Platz" (Hacke's Square). It was

My grandfather was a skilled tobacco mixer[26] and cigarette maker. He had no trouble obtaining a job. Two of his older daughters also found employment in the growing cigarette industry.[27] I do not believe that the Central Committee for Russian Jews ever assisted my family since my grandfather and his two older daughters were able to support the family, albeit rather modestly.

On February 12, 1896, my father (the youngest child and only boy) was born in Berlin. Under the then-existing German law a child born to immigrant parents did not become a German citizen by birth.[28] This strange law (to Americans) incidentally saved him from serving in the

---

named after the same von Hacke who erected the barns. Between 1934 and 1940 I crossed that square every day on my way to school.

[26] My father claimed that my grandfather invented menthol cigarettes by being the first one in Germany to mix cigarette tobacco with menthol. I have no proof for that assertion.

[27] Starting in the late nineteenth century the tobacco workers of Eastern European Jewish background were instrumental in producing those cigarette brands that Berliners preferred most at that time—Garbáty, Manoli and Muratti. Garbáty cigarettes were produced in Berlin's Pankow district. In 2003 a memorial plaque, remembering the cigarette manufacturer Josef Garbáty (1851–1939), was placed at Garbáty Square near the Pankow subway station. The immigrant tobacco workers must have had a worldwide reputation. In 1881 James Buchanan Duke, the later founder of the American Tobacco Co., had entered the cigarette manufacturing business. In his factory in Durham NC, he employed 125 Russian Jewish immigrants.

[28] In commenting upon the election of Gerhard Schröder as the new German Chancellor, *The New York Times* stated on September 29, 1998 in a front-page article that "Germany's immigration laws seem certain to change, reflecting the extent to which this has become a multi-ethnic society. ...This reform... would probably make it possible for immigrants' children born in Germany to gain German citizenship." That actually happened about two years later but with an important exception. Any child born in Germany since January 1, 2000 becomes a German citizen. However, children of parents who are not citizens can only retain such German citizenship after their eighteenth birthday by deciding (until they are 23) to give up any other citizenship they may have inherited from their foreign parents. While I expect this exception will be changed at some time in the future, we have to remember that the original law had survived for more than 100 years.

German Army during World War I. At the beginning of that war, in 1914, he was an 18-year-old native of Germany. Yet, he was born to a father of Russian descent and was therefore declared an "enemy alien." He was never drafted for the Army but was able to work as an electrician. He could have volunteered to serve in the German Army—which he wanted to do in order to join his friends, who were all enthusiastically in favor of the war—but he would have needed the approval of his father since he was less than 21 years old. My grandfather was smart enough to refuse such permission. By 1917 when my father had reached the majority, he had acquired a bride (my parents got married on April 5, 1917) and lost any interest in Army service.

Grandfather continued his work in the tobacco industry until his retirement. He died in Berlin on May 5, 1926. Until the day he died, he lived in the *Scheunenviertel*. My parents and I had left that area in early 1930 when we moved to a new apartment complex in the Weissensee section of Berlin. Four years later and in order to shorten my commutation to the Jewish Middle School, we moved to the center of Berlin where we stayed until our emigration.

My grandfather had never become a German citizen. On April 20, 1932, after years of bureaucratic struggle, my father finally obtained German citizenship for himself, and at the same time for his wife (who had been born in Sadagora, then a part of Austria-Hungary, now in western Ukraine) and for me, a second-generation German-born person.

This hard-fought naturalization was a short-lived one. Among the early laws published by the German Nazi regime was an edict regarding the "Revocation of Naturalization and the Deprivation of German Nationality" which was enacted on July 14, 1933. It took the "efficient" bureaucracy a while but under date of March 27, 1935, my father (and family) lost German citizenship and became what was then called "stateless." (The cancellation document appears in English and in German at the end of this chapter.)

The change in my family's status from German to "stateless" had two important consequences. First, emigration from Germany became even more difficult because there were some countries that continued to accept Jews with German passports, but did not accept stateless persons. The other gave rise to an even more immediate and serious problem. In those early years of the Hitler regime German Jews could legally live and to some extent work in Germany—while stateless ones or those with foreign passports had to apply to the police every six months for permission to stay and to hold a work permit. A law dated March 23, 1934 had declared Germany's right to deport foreign nationals and stateless persons.

Among my father's papers, I found my last extension, dated March 26, 1941, allowing me to stay in Germany until September 12, 1941—18 days *before* the expiration of my school pass. At the same time that Berlin's transit system authority allowed me to travel within the city at a reduced rate, the Nazi government forced us out of Germany. (My extension is shown at the end of this chapter.) I doubt whether a further extension beyond the September date would have been granted. It could have meant that we would have been forcibly transferred to a "camp" in Poland. Most happily, the question never arose because my parents and I were finally able to leave Germany in July 1941.

On May 28, 1938, by order of the State Police and the Ministry of the Interior, a national listing was started of all persons who had lost their German citizenship because of the Revocation of Naturalization Law. The same order also required that the revocation of citizenship be entered in the criminal records (*Die Entziehung der Staatsangehörigkeit ist im Strafregister zu vermerken*). In other words, by losing one's German citizenship—in accordance with a "law" enacted by the Nazis—one was additionally punished by being recorded with convicted criminals. That is just another example of Nazi "justice" at that time.

School Pass Issued by the Berlin Transit Authority (BVG)
(Original donated to the Jewish Museum in Berlin)

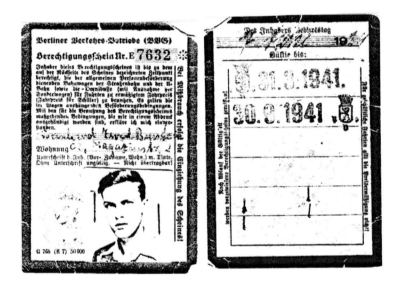

The Chief of Police in Berlin
March 26, 1941
Mr. Bernhard Israel Burstein
Magazinstrasse 2
Berlin C 2

In accordance with your request of March 12, 1941, I grant
you a deadline for your departure until September 12, 1941.

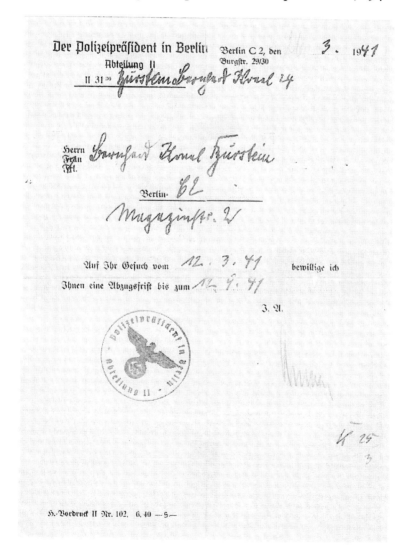

Translation
Cancellation of German Citizenship
(original on the following page)

The Chief of Police
Department II

Berlin, March 27, 1935

Mr. Hermann Burstein
Magazinstrasse 13a
Berlin O 27

<u>Free of Charge!</u>

On April 20, 1932, you had acquired the Prussian nationality by naturalization and thereby became a member of the German Reich. In accordance with paragraph One of the Law regarding the Revocation of Naturalization and the Deprivation of German Nationality, dated July 14, 1933, I hereby revoke this naturalization. This revocation extends also to your wife Rachel, nee Bäcker and the following named member of your family: Bernhard, born on April 7, 1924 in Berlin.

Once you have received this order, you and your aforementioned family members have lost the German nationality and have ceased being members of the German Reich.

This revocation causes—at the same time—the loss of any other naturalization, which you might have acquired in the meantime of another German State.

The revocation cannot be contested by legal redress.

Seal

Signed by
[Signature illegible]

Original
Cancellation of German Citizenship

Der Polizeipräsident
Abteilung II.

Berlin, den 27. März 1935.

Tgb.-Nr. II. 5010. 2929(Ausb.)

An

Herrn Hermann B u r s t e i n

Gebührenfrei!

in B e r l i n O. 27

Magazinstr. 13 a.

Sie haben laut Urkunde vom 20. April 1932 die preußische Staatsangehörigkeit durch Einbürgerung erworben und sind damit deutscher Reichsangehöriger geworden. Gemäß § 1 des Gesetzes über den Widerruf von Einbürgerungen und die Aberkennung der deutschen Staatsangehörigkeit vom 14. Juli 1933 (RGBl. I S. 480) widerrufe ich hiermit diese Einbürgerung. Dieser Widerruf erstreckt sich auf Ihre Ehefrau Rachel, geborene Bäcker und Ihre nachstehend aufgeführten Familienangehörigen:

(Namen) 1. Bernhard, geboren am 7. April 1924 in Berlin

2. — " —

3. — " —

4. — " —

5. — " —

Mit dem Zeitpunkt der Aushändigung dieser Verfügung haben Sie und Ihre vorgenannten Familienangehörigen die preußische deutsche Staatsangehörigkeit verloren und damit aufgehört, deutsche(r) Reichsangehörige(r) zu sein.

Dieser Widerruf bewirkt zugleich den Verlust jeder, also auch einer inzwischen durch Aufnahme hinzuerworbenen Staatsangehörigkeit eines anderen deutschen Landes.

Der Widerruf kann nicht mit Rechtsmitteln angefochten werden.

In Vertretung:

(Siegel)

N. 61. Widerruf der Einbürgerung.

5

"Visiting" Carin Hall

A LENGTHY ARTICLE in the January 21, 1990 edition of *The New York Times Book Review* caught my eye. Written by Ella Leffland and entitled "Has Anybody Seen Göring?" it described the author's travels through post-war Germany researching her then soon-to-be-published novel *The Knight, Death and the Devil*. The novel was based on the life of Hermann Göring, the second highest official in Nazi Germany and at one time the designated successor to Hitler.

Several years before the beginning of the war, Göring had built an imposing hunting lodge in the Schorfheide region, about 39 miles NNE of Berlin. He named the compound "Carin Hall" after his late first wife, the Swedish aristocrat Baroness Carin von Fock-Kantzow. The entire place was destroyed in 1945.

Again, as I read the article old memories came to mind. As I had previously indicated, my parents were not wealthy at all. With one single exception, around 1930, I do not recall that we ever took a "real" vacation while in Germany. Instead, as long as it was possible, until about summer 1938, my parents rented a room with kitchen facilities near one of the many lakes surrounding Berlin. My mother and I spent about four to six weeks during the summer school vacations at that place, with my father visiting us on weekends and during his own vacations.

Since my mother and I did not "look Jewish," we were able to find such an accommodation among the farmers who were anxious to rent a room during the vacation time.

One summer we spent somewhere in the Schorfheide region. I have no recollection regarding the actual site. I believe it must have been in either 1935 or 1936, i.e. when I was 11 or 12 years old. Having heard about Carin Hall, I was intrigued to see the place for myself. I then embarked upon a potentially dangerous and at the very least extremely stupid mission.

One morning, without telling my mother, I took my bicycle and traveled in the direction of Carin Hall. I was certain that I would not be able to enter the place through the main gate. Therefore, I parked my bicycle on a side road and then started to climb a small hill, which I believed would allow me to view Göring's "castle."

Having climbed for a short while, I noticed evenly spread wires on the ground, which I took as some type of an early warning system. I did not wait to find out, but raced down to my bicycle and pedaled back to the place we had rented. I never did see Carin Hall nor did I ever discuss this adventure with anyone.

Within a few days after I had read her article, I wrote to Ella Leffland and described to her my childish prank. Shortly thereafter, I received her answer. I am quoting a paragraph of Ms. Leffland's letter:

> When you say, "I hope these memories are not too boring," I must say they are the exact opposite—fascinating and stimulating. I naturally felt, when undertaking to write such a book as *The Knight, Death and the Devil*, that I had some kind of strong, inexplicable affinity with the place and the period (or else I would never have had the effrontery to put down a word); but I know there is

no comparison between someone who was not there (despite all the affinity in the world) and someone who was. I would therefore be extremely interested and grateful, if you would write me your response to the book. Again, I thank you so much for sharing your experiences of these far-off days.

Reading Ms. Leffland's novel, I was amazed by the way in which she wove "real" people like Göring and Goebbels etc. together with imaginary characters. This is, of course, not new in the world of literature. However, I thought it was rather well put together in her book. Here is an excerpt of my review, which I sent to Ms. Leffland:

> The book shows an amazing insight into the situation in Germany as I personally experienced. Nikki and Hans Schmidt, Rose and Max Korwan and even Frau Kloppmann and her family are just like actual people I have known. The struggle of German Jewry is accurately described—as if you had really lived there during that time. You have left nothing out—neither the curfew that was only disseminated by word of mouth (and broken many times by myself); not even the fact that Voss and Wilhelmstrasse were forbidden territory for Jews.[29]

---

[29] A secret notification to the German press, dated September 15, 1939, read as follows: "Foreign newspapers have declared that Jews in Germany are not allowed to be outside their homes after 8 PM. This is correct. All police districts have issued these instructions. These rules became necessary because Jews have frequently used the (wartime) blackout requirements to molest Aryan women." (In reality all Jewish communities had been "advised" on September 1, 1939 to inform their members that Jews must be staying at their homes after 8 PM.) In the chapter "My Middle Name Was Israel And Other Indignities," I have discussed the edict prohibiting Jews from walking on certain streets in Berlin even during daytime hours.

The despair after World War I, the steady emergence of nationalistic feelings, the reaction to Hitlerism is all explained in such a way that I had to put the book down, from time to time; too many memories suddenly cropped up. All in all, a fascinating description of a tragic era in German (and world) history extremely well researched. Reading *The Knight, Death and the Devil* was a bittersweet enjoyment.

The "memories" I mentioned referred to the later period under Hitler. I was barely nine years old when Hitler assumed power and I was too young to have developed any nationalistic or pro-German feelings. I really had no conception as a child of what was going on. The nationalism and the "despair" that I mentioned was something I only read about and became aware of at a later time. However, the writer, an American, had described what went on in Germany in such a vivid way that it touched and saddened me deeply.

6

Der Jüdische Kulturbund (The Jewish Culture League)

BOTH MY PARENTS liked to see operas. In spite of their financial situation, they always seemed to have managed to attend several opera performances during the season; usually at one of the two major opera houses in Berlin, the State Opera and the City Opera (now called the German Opera).

They were interested in the entire repertoire of these houses, equally enthusiastic about Mozart, Offenbach, Verdi or Wagner, just to name a few of their favorite composers. My paternal grandfather—who had taken Papa to see performances from about his fifteenth birthday—had introduced him to the opera. On many occasions, Papa would tell me that his greatest thrill of an opera performance came rather early in his life. Around 1912 or 1913, Enrico Caruso, considered to this day as perhaps the greatest tenor of the twentieth century, sang at the Prussian State Opera. The German emperor Wilhelm II attended that performance. Papa and his father had seats somewhere in the upper ranks on the same evening. This was a wonderful operatic and political highlight for him. (Papa even mentioned that the performance had started a few minutes late—unheard of in punctual Prussia—because the Kaiser was delayed.)

Around my tenth birthday, I started taking piano lessons given by a Fräulein Lieblich. She was a rather pleasant young woman, probably a decent pianist but without much educational experience. After about a year, she told my mother to discontinue the lessons because I did not practice hard enough. She was essentially correct. I wonder, however, whether she could have used some better methods to entice me to practice. Some 40 years later my late friend Kurt Ingwer recalled that my mother would not allow us to play together until I had finished practicing. He claimed to have enjoyed my piano playing—but perhaps he was too polite to tell me the truth. Sadly, we shall never know.

Before discontinuing the lessons, I was on my second or third piano practice book and the only music I played consisted of short operatic excerpts. When I was about twelve years old, I received, as a Hanukkah gift, my first record player together with about six or eight records, all of them excerpts from operas. I distinctly remember that two of those records contained music by Wagner.

Five extremely difficult years later—and within three months after I had left Germany—I attended a midnight concert by the Havana Philharmonic Orchestra led by the guest conductor Erich Kleiber, himself a refugee from Nazi Germany. (I had bought a ticket for the midnight concert because I could not afford the price for the regular evening performance.) The only music I remember from that concert was Ravel's *Bolero*. At that moment it became the most emotionally satisfying music I had ever heard. It showed me that there was "something else" beyond opera and enhanced my interest and love for music. I do not recall that my parents ever acknowledged an affinity for any music other than the classic opera.

Their enthusiasm for attending opera performances began to cool with the onset of the Hitler regime, regardless of the fact that it was not yet prohibited for Jews. That "only" happened in December 1938, as I have described more fully in the chapter entitled "My Middle Name Was Israel and Other Indignities." However, the atmosphere had changed and my parents were uncomfortable, to say the least, in going to the opera and sitting next to more and more people wearing Nazi membership insignias or even uniforms. They felt out of place and, I would think, rather frightened. Then a new chapter opened for Jews in Berlin.

Shortly after January 30, 1933, all Jewish artists were dismissed from all theaters, opera houses and orchestras throughout Germany. Many, particularly the more prominent ones, left the country. However, other hundreds were suddenly facing unemployment. In July 1933 the Jewish community in Berlin (and later on in other cities in Germany) formed a Jewish "Culture League"— Kulturbund—and received permission from the Nazi propaganda ministry to perform "for Jews only" a variety of theater performances, operas and concerts. As this league took hold, it added children's and youth performances and even a movie theater.

It did mean a relatively decent income for some of the Jewish artists living in Germany and allowed the Jewish public to forget for a few fleeting hours the ever-tightening noose. However, it forced the managers of the league to coordinate their activities with the Nazis and it gave the regime a propaganda weapon to "prove" that the Jews in Germany were free to run their own theaters and other cultural activities and were able to afford these "luxuries." Attendance at any performance of the Kulturbund was strictly regulated. You had to be a member of the association and declare that you were Jewish. Non-Jews were prohibited from attending any of its performances. I have donated my membership certificate to the Jewish Museum in Berlin.

The performances under the original name of *Kulturbund deutscher Juden* (Culture League of German Jews) began on October 1, 1933. Within two years, the organization was forced by the Nazis to change its name to *Jüdischer Kulturbund in Deutschland* (Jewish Culture League in Germany). The implication of having *German* Jews became too difficult for them to swallow.

Around 1935 there existed about 36 Jewish culture leagues in about 100 cities throughout Germany. Most of these local groups were required to discontinue their work following the Kristallnacht in November 1938. By order of Dr. Goebbels, the Kulturbund in Berlin, however, was forced to restart its performances on November 20 of that year for purely propagandistic reasons.

That latter organization existed until September 11, 1941 when it had lost its propaganda value to the Nazis and was dissolved by government fiat. Its funds were confiscated and the remaining artists and staff were sent to various concentration and extermination camps. Another dream of "German" Jews had ended.[30]

My first operatic experience was at the Kulturbund. In October or November 1935 my friend Kurt Ingwer and I saw Rossini's *The Barber of Seville*, sung in German. I was thrilled. On October 31, 1935 the *C.V. Zeitung*, a German-Jewish newspaper, reviewed the performance and gave it extremely high marks. The paper ended with this thoughtful observation: "The Kulturbund's performance, full of liveliness, good mood and real ensemble spirit will carry this wonderful atmosphere into our everyday life!"

---

[30] See also Martin Goldsmith, *The Inextinguishable Symphony: A True Story of Music and Love in Nazi Germany*. New York: John Wiley & Sons, 2000. The parents of the author were active members of the Kulturbund.

Unfortunately, people had not yet realized what was in store for them.

I have seen *The Barber of Seville* on several occasions since then, the last time—as of this writing—at the Metropolitan Opera in New York in November 2009. This opera still has a special place in my heart.

7

The Jewish Hospital in Berlin and My First Encounter With Women's Equality

I WAS A very active sports enthusiast in my younger years. I believe it was 1938 when I participated in the last sports festival of all Jewish schools in Berlin. I placed sixth in a three-part competition (100m sprint, long jump and shot put). I do not remember the results of that competition except that I ran the 100m sprint in about 13.6 seconds; not exactly a world record at that time (10.3 seconds) but still a respectable accomplishment for a 14-year-old boy. I also anchored the final leg of the victorious 4x100-meter relay team.

In late spring of 1940, I had an accident while high jumping (diagnosis: bilateral hernia). Consequently, in July I was a patient at the Jewish Hospital and underwent surgical repair.[31] In my November 1941 letter to Harry Pomeranz, I discussed this hospital stay. I told him about a shortage of milk, a lack of castor oil, that the bandages consisted partially of paper and that there was a shortage

---

[31] The surgeon who operated on me was Dr. Ernst Eylenburg. He was first deported to Theresienstadt on August 4, 1943 and from there with one of the last transports on October 19, 1944 to Auschwitz, where he perished.

of iodine. I also stated that iodine was unavailable even on the "black market." I have no idea why I should have been so concerned regarding the availability of iodine.

Medically I was well-treated at the hospital, where I spent a little more than two weeks recovering from the operation. I understand that nowadays a bilateral hernia operation is performed on an outpatient basis.

During my recovery my parents, friends and relatives visited me. Another person saw me daily outside the regular visitors' hours. She was a young woman (I later found out she was then about 38 years old) who had introduced herself, I believe, as "Frau Rabbiner Jonas" (Rabbi Jonas). She arrived usually by mid-morning and visited many of the patients in the hospital. As best as I am able to recollect she usually spent several minutes talking to me. Up to that time, I had never heard anything about her. Yet I do remember her full name, Regina Jonas.

An article, headlined "Furor in Germany over Female Rabbi," appeared on August 2, 1995 in *The New York Times*. In short, it discussed that a Swiss woman, Bea Wyler, had become Germany's first female rabbi, having been appointed by the congregations in Oldenburg and Braunschweig (Lower Saxony). These appointments had been sharply criticized by Ignatz Bubis, an Orthodox Jew who at that time headed the Central Council of Jews in Germany. Bubis went so far as to say he would not attend any worship service let by Rabbi Wyler! In reply, the chairperson of the Oldenburg congregation stated that by choosing a woman rabbi, the congregation was bringing an older tradition back to Germany. Before World War II, there was rabbinical education for women in Germany and there had been a woman rabbi, Regina Jonas.

A letter to the editor of *The New York Times*, published on August 12, replied to the above-mentioned article.

German Woman Rabbi

To the Editor:

Your Aug. 2 news article on a female rabbi in Germany quotes Sara-Ruth Schumann, chairwoman of the Oldenberg congregation, as saying that before World War II in Germany, "there was a woman rabbi, Regina Jonas."

While Ms. Jonas undertook rabbinical studies in the mid-1930's at the Berlin Academy for the Science of Judaism, she was not ordained there, primarily because of the opposition of a Talmud professor.

An individual rabbi, Max Dienemann of Offenbach, did ordain her, but she apparently never served a congregation. She was deported to Theresienstadt and died, or was killed, during the Holocaust.

Rabbi Bea Wyler, around whom controversy swirls, was ordained by the Jewish Theological Seminary of America and will be the first female rabbi engaged by a German synagogue.　　ANNE LAPIDUS LERNER
Vice Chancellor, Jewish
Theological Seminary of America
New York, Aug. 7, 1995

That letter prompted me to write directly to Dr. Lerner. I mentioned my background, my hospital stay, and the visits by Rabbi Jonas.[32] I also enclosed an early draft of

---

[32] Dr. Lerner correctly pointed out that Regina Jonas studied for the rabbinate in Berlin. She was a student at the College for the Scientific Study of Judaism, previously mentioned in my chapter "The Shipment to Switzerland." While she had passed all her exams, she was not ordained a rabbi because of the opposition of the professor of Talmud and Rabbinics, who was the only one authorized to sign the diploma of

"A Letter to my Grandchildren," which now appears at the beginning of this book, because it touches upon my personal experiences in Nazi Germany and coincides with the time that I had met that wonderful human being, Rabbi Jonas. I ended my letter to Dr. Lerner stating, "Rabbi Jonas may not have had a congregation but she certainly helped me and countless others at an abnormal time."

Dr. Lerner very graciously acknowledged my writing to her. I am reprinting her answer in full at the end of this chapter; the text appears also on pages 187–188. In trying to answer the questions Dr. Lerner asked me, I pointed out that purely by chance, the same week I received her letter I became aware that a German Jewish weekly (*Allgemeine Jüdische Wochenzeitschrift*) had published an article about Regina Jonas, and had

---

ordination. He had categorically refused to sign the diploma and had stated "I am not going to ordain a girl." Her private ordination came several years later through Rabbi Dienemann as stated in the above-cited letter to the editor. (See also *Hochschule Retrospective* by Dr. Alexander Guttmann, published by *CCAR Journal*, Autumn 1972 under the auspices of the Central Conference of American Rabbis, New York, NY.) In her thesis "Can a Woman Hold Rabbinical Office?" Regina Jonas had argued that true Judaism is egalitarian in nature since God would never oppress a human being. She also stated that most of the practices in Judaism which exclude women were historical developments due to patriarchal attitudes not inherent to Judaism. (See also David J. Fine, *Weekly Chronicle*, Office of Student Life, Jewish Theological Seminary of America, New York, NY, Volume XIII, Issue 5, November 21, 1994.) The Leo Baeck Institute published an extensive essay about Rabbi Jonas, written by Katharina von Kellerbach, *Year Book 1994* (Martin Secker & Warburg Limited, London), entitled "God Does Not Oppress Any Human Being." Ms. von Kellerbach also quoted from Jonas's thesis: "The world after all consists of two genders due to God and it cannot in the long run be supported by only one gender."

It should be noted that Jonas's thesis was written in 1930 in pre-Hitler Germany. She was definitely ahead of her time. The thesis, edited and with extensive commentary and well-researched by Elisa Klapheck, was finally published under the title *Fräulein Rabbiner Jonas. Kann eine Frau das rabbinische Amt bekleiden?* (Miss Rabbi Jonas. Can a Woman Hold Rabbinical Office?) Teetz, Germany: Hentrich & Hentrich, 1999. As of this writing, however, this book is only available in German.

mentioned that she was deported to Auschwitz in October 1944, probably with the last train from Theresienstadt.

I also told Dr. Lerner that I did not remember much of my meetings with Rabbi Jonas. It was easy, however, for me to accept the fact of a woman being a rabbi, having grown up in a family where my mother was the dominant intellectual person. My mother's reaction—as I recall—was quite different. She had come from an Orthodox home and thought it was weird, almost blasphemous, that a woman should be considered a rabbi.

I also mentioned in my reply to Dr. Lerner that I personally believe that the ability to deal with the then-existing situation in an optimistic fashion had helped me. Had I known of extermination or slave labor camps, I likely would have found it more difficult to remain optimistic.

Later I had the pleasure of meeting Dr. Lerner personally. In discussing my background with her, I found out that her family came from the same general area in Tsarist Russia as my paternal one. It is a small world indeed.

Letter from Dr. Lerner
(text also appears on pages 187–188)

AND THE BUSH הסנה
WAS NOT איננו
CONSUMED אכל

27 AV 5755
August 23, 1995

THE JEWISH
THEOLOGICAL
SEMINARY
OF AMERICA

3080 Broadway
New York, NY 10027-4649
(212) 678-8000

FAX (212) 678-8947

Office of the
Vice-Chancellor
(212) 678-8069

Mr. Bernard Burton
142 Monterey Drive
Manhasset Hills, NY 11040

Dear Mr. Burton:

I am moved beyond words by your letter to me and by the copy of the letter to your grandchildren you so generously shared with me.

Rabbi Jonas has been of interest to me for many years. As one who has been deeply involved in opening the rabbinate to women, I often wondered what became of her. Yours is the only testimony I have from a person whose life she touched. I would love to know what you thought at the time. Was having a woman introduce herself that way not perceived as strange?

The letter for your grandchildren was deeply moving, particularly because it is so spare and factual. It is hard for me to imagine, from the vantage point of the security of Jewish life in late twentieth century New York, how one came through these times. Was survival supported by the ability to deal with the situation in optimistic fashion? The miracle of you and your father finding yourselves just outside the emigration ban is amazing.

I hope that you will choose to share your letter with some of the institutions which collect Holocaust memories. It is extremely moving.

May God grant you and yours a year of health, peace and fulfillment.

Sincerely,

Dr. Anne Lapidus Lerner
Vice Chancellor

בית המדרש לרבנים באמריקה

This is a picture of the last Sports Festival of Jewish Schools in Berlin, probably summer of 1938. I am in the middle of the first row, looking down. An enlarged copy of this picture hangs prominently today in the lobby of the *Jüdische Oberschule* (Jewish High School), the successor to the Middle School from which I graduated in 1940. The present high school has operated since 1996.

The Jewish Community of Berlin owned a sports stadium in the Grunewald section. An order, dated August 31, 1935, stated in part that Jewish sports organizations are not to be disturbed until new laws are issued *after* the Olympic Games. The order further mentioned that such regulations were necessary to prevent the Olympic Games from being transferred to another country because of "anti-German propaganda." However, a prior regulation of July 10, 1935 prohibited walks or hikes by Jewish youth groups in excess of 20 people.

The Gestapo confiscated Berlin's Jewish sports complex at the end of 1938.

8

My Middle Name Was Israel and Other Indignities

A DECREE OF August 17, 1938 proclaimed that Jewish children born after that date may only be given names listed in the "guidelines" issued by the Reich Minister of the Interior. Jews who had been given names other than those on the "approved" list were obligated, as of January 1, 1939, to assume as an additional given name "Israel" for males and "Sara" for females.

A courageous article printed on September 1, 1938 in the *C.V. Zeitung*, one of the few Jewish newspapers still being published in Berlin and from which I have previously quoted, explained the meaning of the name Israel. Without referring to the law of August 17 it quoted the Holy Scriptures (Genesis 32:29) "...Your name shall no longer be Jacob, but Israel, for you have striven with beings divine and human, and have prevailed" (...*nicht Jakob soll fortan sein Name heissen, sondern Israel, denn Du hast mit Gott und Menschen gekämpft und hast gesiegt*).[33]

The approved list of Jewish names consisted of 185 male and 95 female first names. To a great degree, the

---

[33] See also Herbert Freeden, *Die jüdische Presse im Dritten Reich*. Frankfurt/M:Jüdischer Verlag bei Athenäum, 1987. English translation of the biblical passage: *Tanakh, The Holy Scriptures*. Philadelphia: The Jewish Publication Society, 1985.

names selected sounded strange or even repulsive to the average German; hence—in my opinion—their inclusion in the list. Rereading the compilation now, I find it surprising that male first names like Dan, Denny, Joel or Noa and female names such as Abigail, Rachel and Rebekka had been included as Jewish.[34] On the other hand, while Moses was considered a Jewish name, Abraham and Jakob were not.

A further requirement of this law dictated that the names Israel or Sara, respectively, had to be spelled out in any document or public paper, including, for example, the return address on an envelope.

The forced addition of the name Israel was to me personally perhaps the harshest law of the Nazi period between 1933 and the date of my emigration in July 1941. I do not want to be misunderstood. There were, unfortunately, many more laws that were worse than having to state, in effect, any time you signed your name or showed your identity card, that you were Jewish. There were laws that affected the economic well-being or dignity of a person. Other laws excluded Jews from any type of activity with non-Jews. However, I was a child when Hitler came to power and only a teenager when I left Germany. Most of these laws, while I may have been aware of them, did not affect me on a daily basis. This one did, and therefore had a devastating effect on me.

As of September 1, 1939 (the beginning of the war), a new requirement was put into force. *All* mail to a foreign country had to carry a verified return address and had to have the postage affixed at a post office by a postal employee. That law applied to all remitters of mail to a foreign country. I do believe this was a security measure to

---

[34] For more details and a complete list see Hartmut Jäckel/Hermann Simon, *Berliner Juden 1941*. Teetz: Verlag Hentrich & Hentrich, 2007.

avoid having any additional message concealed under the stamp/s. It effectively made the sender responsible for the contents of the letter.

Between September 1939 and July 1941, I mailed letters to the USA and to my friend Harry Pomeranz in Uruguay. I never had any problem at the post office and all letters arrived at their destinations (after having passed German censorship). My experience mailing letters, however, was strictly in Berlin. I understand that outside of Berlin Jews may have been treated differently. For example, Barth Healey, a *New York Times* columnist with whom I corresponded briefly after he wrote about these matters in his column,[35] stated to me in a note that "... it is common thought that postal clerks were often asked to take special note of mail sent by Jews." This was easy because the envelope itself indicated whether the sender was Jewish.

It is a well-known fact that people have different pain thresholds. Therefore, it should not be surprising that many of us in Germany had different thoughts and opinions regarding the severity of the anti-Jewish laws that had been thrust upon us. I mentioned that the addition of Israel to my name was a tremendous shock to me. My mother—who incidentally did not need to add the name Sara because her given name Rachel was an "approved" Jewish name—reacted quite differently. As far as I remember, nothing seemed to upset her outwardly, not even the unemployment of my father, which I shall discuss. In retrospect she probably was extremely upset with everything that was going on. However, she never let me

---

[35] Between 1988 and 1993, Barth Healey wrote a *New York Times* column entitled "Stamps." The column that began our correspondence appeared in the Sunday, March 22, 1992 edition of *The New York Times*, and discussed the philatelic evidence of the anti-Semitic acts perpetrated by the Nazis.

feel it, but constantly tried to shield me from the unpleasant surroundings. I am sure she suffered more than I ever will know. I had mentioned earlier that I considered her the "intellectual" head of the family. She was doubtless more aware of what was happening than my father but she was careful to protect her "Berndchen" (little Bernie). I do believe the addition of Israel as a required middle name was probably by itself not as much of a calamity to my mother as it was to me. She may have sensed that worse laws were going to follow.

However, she too had a pain threshold! On November 28, 1938, an order of the State Police gave local authorities the "right" to restrict Jews from entering certain areas of a city or district and/or to disallow them to visit any area at specified times. (Police Order regarding the appearance of Jews in public.—*Polizeiverordnung über das Auftreten der Juden in der Öffentlichkeit*.)

Following up on that order, as of December 6, 1938, Jews were prohibited throughout Germany to visit theaters, opera or movie houses, cabarets, public concerts, libraries, museums, places of entertainment, exhibition halls, sporting events, ice-skating rinks, public baths or bathing or other recreational facilities. Entering restaurants or other eating facilities was not prohibited at that time but the majority of restaurants (if not all) had posted signs for many years stating "Jews Not Welcome" (*Juden Unerwünscht*), "Jews Prohibited" (*Juden Verboten*), or even "Jews and Dogs Prohibited" (*Juden und Hunde Verboten*). Until my emigration, Berlin had, as far as I remember, two Jewish-owned restaurants "For Jews Only" (*Nur für Juden*).[36]

---

[36] In this connection I note an order, dated December 3, 1935, which read as follows: "In order not to jeopardize the Olympic Games of 1936 in Berlin, all anti-Jewish signs and placards in the area of Garmisch-Partenkirchen [host city for the Olympic Winter Games] have to be

Additionally, in Berlin, Jews were prohibited from walking on certain streets (Wilhelmstrasse from the corner of Leipziger Strasse up to Unter den Linden; Vossstrasse up to Wilhelmstrasse, in front of Hitler's Chancellery; and the northern side of Unter den Linden, from the university to the Zeughaus, or Weapons Museum). The areas now prohibited to be entered by Jews contained streets where major government offices and the Tomb of the Unknown Soldier were located (though for many years, most Jews had shied away from being seen in that area in any case, unless it was essential). These new restrictions were covered by a word that was new to me: *Judenbann* (banishment of Jews).

This new law had a profound effect on my mother. I saw her crying for the first time and she was talking about committing suicide. From then until we left Germany, I was always afraid that she would actually hold to that threat.

I have no knowledge or recollection of which law or laws my father might have considered the worst, since we

---

removed." A more general order, dated June 11, 1936, read: "On account of the Olympic Games signs stating 'Jews Not Welcome' and similar descriptions are to be removed discreetly from the main thoroughfares" (*Tafeln Juden unerwünscht und ähnliche sind von den Hauptstrassen (wegen der Olympiade) unauffällig zu entfernen*). I have already mentioned that Jewish sports organizations were also left undisturbed until after the Olympic Games.

The late American writer and journalist William L. Shirer described that (he) "was violently attacked in the German press and on the radio, and threatened with expulsion, for having written a dispatch saying that some of these anti-Semitic signs were being removed for the duration of the Olympic Games." See also page 234 of *The Rise and Fall of the Third Reich*. (New York: Simon and Schuster, 1960)

On June 23, 1936 a Nazi order under the title "Prohibition of all physical violence towards foreigners and Jews" (*Verbot aller Tätlichkeiten gegen Ausländer und Juden*) stated in part that "... because of the Olympic Games from August 1 to August 16, 1936 the SS is prohibited from engaging in such violent acts..." It is almost unbelievable that a "law" had to be enacted to prohibit the beating of foreigners and Jews during the Olympic Games.

never talked about it. Previously I had alluded to the fact that he lost his job on July 19, 1938, and I have copied his letter of dismissal at the end of this chapter. The "interesting" part of that letter is the reason given for the discharge. It was called "reorganization of the business." There was no reorganization at all, but even at that late date, hardly any dismissal notice given to a Jew would ever tell the truth. If it was not reorganization then it might be called "voluntary separation," or by a similar innocuous phrase. Incidentally, Papa was the last Jewish employee to be dismissed by the company.

Gebr. Kleinmann

Fernsprecher
Sammelnummer
Lichtenberg 55 5451
Postscheck-Konto No. 79142
Bank-Konto
Dresdner Bank Dep. Kasse 77
Reinhardtst.

Berlin-Lichtenberg, den 19. 7. 38
Wilhelmstr. 21

Z e u g n i s !

Herr Hermann Burstein war vom 19.1.31 bis 19.7.38 als Elektriker bei uns beschäftigt. In dieser Eigenschaft hat er die ihm übertragenen Arbeiten zu unserer vollsten Zufriedenheit ausgeführt. Wir haben Herrn Burstein dann später in unser Materiallager übernommen, wo er sich ebenfalls durch Umsicht und Fleiss das Vertrauen seiner Vorgesetzten erworben hat.
Wir entlassen Herrn Burstein mit dem heutigen Tage wegen Umorganisation des Betriebes.

Gebr. Kleinmann
Berlin-Lichtenberg
Betriebsleitung

Reference

Mr. Hermann Burstein has been employed by us as an electrician from 1/19/31 to 7/19/38. In this capacity he has handled his job to our complete satisfaction. We later transferred Mr. Burstein to our raw material department where he also gained the trust of his superiors by working with discretion and diligence.
We discharge Mr. Burstein as of today because of reorganization of the business.

9

Crystal Night—November 1938

In Memory of "Aunt Dora"

THE SO-CALLED *Reichskristallnacht* (Crystal Night) of November 9 to 10, 1938, and the days and weeks following that event, definitely formed the most vicious anti-Jewish period of the *pre-war* Hitler regime. In writing about my own feelings and observations regarding this event, one important point has to be kept in mind. This event "played out" differently in the various cities and villages of Germany and Austria (which had become, in March 1938, a part of "Greater Germany"). Whatever I observed was limited to a narrow center of Berlin. Nothing I have written should be considered applicable to the entire country or even to greater Berlin itself.

Previously I had mentioned that my parents were not wealthy. Considering my present standard of living, I should say they were poor. I refer to their economic status because it influenced my knowledge (or lack of it) of the upcoming catastrophe and had a direct bearing on how this unspeakable period affected my parents and me.

A German law—predating and unrelated to the Nazis—required anyone having a radio to pay a monthly fee to the postal system for the privilege of using it. Until around 1934, we had a radio in our apartment. Then my parents sold it and from then on saved the listeners' fee.[37] At about the same time they also canceled their subscription to a daily newspaper. The only paper that continued to arrive at our house was the weekly edition of the *Jüdisches Gemeindeblatt* (Jewish Community Paper).

Telephone service was generally available throughout Germany. Naturally, the percentage of households with telephones was substantially lower than at the present time. Most of my parents' friends and relatives had telephone service in their apartments. Yet, we never subscribed to it—again, I would imagine, for economic reasons. If I wanted to call a friend once I had left school, I would walk to the nearest post office—about a block away from our apartment—and use the public telephone.

However, by that time, as I recall, people would not talk freely by telephone, fearing that the dreaded Gestapo was listening to calls made by Jews. I have no knowledge of the existence of such a listening system but the mere fact that people believed they were being overheard made them more cautious when making telephone calls.

Let me first briefly recap the historical sequence that brought about the "Crystal Night" calamity.

On October 28, 1938 (and I remember that date well because it was my mother's forty-first birthday) we were completely taken by surprise. In early morning raids the police arrested all male Jews (throughout Germany) above the age of 15 who either had Polish citizenship, were stateless but had been born in Poland, or were the sons of Polish fathers (although they themselves may have been born in Germany). I remember that a number of my fellow

---

[37] Starting on January 9, 1934, the German government discontinued any commercial advertising via radio. An order of September 23, 1939 required that all radio equipment owned by Jews be turned over, without compensation, to the local police precincts.

classmates did not show up in school that morning. They had been arrested and I never saw them again.

All these unfortunate people (estimated at about 15,000) were taken by trains and forcibly expelled from Germany by being literally dumped at the Polish border. They were left without food or water. I understand that quite a few men died before they finally made it to Poland where they were not particularly welcomed either!

Among the expellees was Zindel Grynszpan. The latter had earlier sent his 17-year-old boy Herschel to live with Zindel's brother in Paris. When Herschel heard, several days later, what had happened to his father in Germany, he went berserk. He walked into the German embassy on November 7 and shot Herr Ernst vom Rath, a third secretary, who died two days later. During the later trial in France, it was determined that Grynszpan had not known vom Rath. The latter was simply the first official Herschel encountered at the embassy, since the German ambassador had refused to see him. Grynszpan was sentenced to prison. When Germany overran France in 1940, he was taken out of jail and turned over to the Germans. He did not survive the war.

This "unprovoked" shooting provided Hitler, Goebbels and his other henchmen with the probably long-awaited opportunity to incite Germans to rise "spontaneously" in bloody vengeance against the Jews. They portrayed the killing of Herr vom Rath not as an act by a desperate Jewish kid, but as a conspiracy by "International Jewry."

On the morning of November 10, 1938, I went to school as usual. I may not even have known that vom Rath had died the previous afternoon. On my way, I passed two small (Jewish) retail stores whose windows were broken. Some of the goods in the stores had also been damaged. There was no looting. I did not pay any particular attention to these stores and did not connect them with any broader anti-Jewish measure. The only brief thought that crossed my mind was the fact that it was extremely rare to see a broken window in a store in Berlin, and now I had seen two in short succession.

It was not until I reached the school (which had not been damaged except that the bust of Moses Mendelssohn in front of the school building had been smashed) that I heard from some of my classmates and teachers what was happening. Attendance at school was low. I had mentioned earlier that we had lost students on October 28. Now perhaps only half the remaining students showed up. Several male teachers did not attend either; they had been arrested during the night, and, as we found out later, taken to the Sachsenhausen concentration camp near Berlin.

It was also in school that I was told that the synagogue at Kaiser-Strasse (around the corner from our apartment) had been severely vandalized. It was not burned because of its location in an apartment complex; a fire would have seriously damaged "Aryan property." This was the same synagogue where I had celebrated my Bar Mitzvah about a year and a half earlier. The synagogue was never used again. Later, during the war, air raids destroyed the entire area. When rebuilding started, in the post-war era, that part of the city was reconfigured and even the street has now disappeared. One reason, in my opinion, for the heavy destruction may have been the fact that the synagogue was located only a few hundred feet from the main police station of Berlin.

The school officials who were present decided not to hold any regular classes. About an hour or two after I had arrived, we were instructed to leave the school and to return directly to our respective homes. We were also advised to leave alone or in very small groups—and my friend Harry and I left together. We went a slightly different route from the one I had taken in the morning, and we passed several more damaged Jewish stores. Yet I did not see any looting or other physical violence. Neither Harry nor I had any problem in getting home.

It was probably around 11:00 in the morning when I returned to our apartment. My mother was extremely happy to see me but also highly agitated. In order to explain the cause for her nervous behavior I have to digress so one will better understand the circumstances.

In a subsequent chapter, I have made the statement that by 1934 all of my parents' non-Jewish friends had deserted us. There was only one welcome exception. Frau Dora Doss, or Tante (Aunt) Dora, as I called her, was an old friend of my father's sister. She was a wonderful person. After my own aunt emigrated in early 1934, Aunt Dora continued to visit us several times a year. She always came unannounced and never stayed at our place for more than 30 or 40 minutes, always afraid that someone might have followed and would denounce her for keeping up a friendship with Jews. She never came without presents! During the early war years, these presents consisted of items that were no longer readily available to Jews, such as tea, soap or fruit. She constantly admonished my parents and tried to convince them to leave Germany as soon as possible, because, as she pleaded, "things were only going to get worse for Jews."

On November 10, 1938, after I had left for school, Aunt Dora had suddenly appeared at our apartment to advise my father that she had received "creditable information" that male Jews were being arrested during the next several days to be sent to concentration camps. She strongly suggested that he immediately go into hiding at his older sister's apartment, because that sister, a widow, had no male person registered to live there. Therefore, neither the police nor the Gestapo was likely to look for him at that place. This brave German Christian woman literally risked her life to conspire with a Jewish man to try to keep him out of the clutches of the Nazis. The strange part of this story is the fact that neither my parents nor I really knew anything about her (except that she had been my aunt's best friend). We had never been to her apartment, nor had we ever met any of her relatives.

When my mother related Aunt Dora's visit and the latter's concern to me—while my father was getting ready to leave our apartment for that of his older sister (Aunt Therese)—I thought the "creditable information" Aunt Dora had been talking about was a figment of her imagination.

Later, I have sadly come to understand that Aunt Dora really must have had some important connections. The information she shared certainly did not appear in any newspaper nor was it broadcast on the radio.

Aunt Dora continued visiting us until July 1941, a few days before our emigration. In a previous chapter, "The Shipment to Switzerland," I described the difficulty in taking books out of Germany. At Aunt Dora's suggestion at her last visit, I turned over to her my beginner's stamp album and two or three books that I particularly liked. She promised to hold these items for me until "Hitler was gone." Incidentally, the stamp album was a gift from my cousin Miriam before her emigration to Palestine around the beginning of 1938. At that time, Miriam had not been able to take the album with her either.

On page 86, I reprinted the U.S. Army Order permitting me to visit Berlin in November 1947. A day after my arrival I started a search for Aunt Dora. I only remembered the name of her street but not the house number. Therefore, I went to the nearest police station in that area, trying to find out her whereabouts. Arriving at the precinct, I saw a line of easily 50–75 German civilians all equally searching for friends or relatives, stoically awaiting their turn to talk to the only police officer who handled these inquiries. I realized that it might possibly take several hours to be able to contact him.

However, this was Berlin in 1947! Here I was a U.S. non-commissioned officer in the American sector of Berlin. I simply walked up to the head of the line and within a few minutes, I had the answer I was seeking from a German police officer who stood at attention when he talked to me. He not only had found the address of Frau Dora Doss but also explained in detail how to reach her apartment house.

Before leaving for Berlin, I had remembered that Aunt Dora liked to drink strong coffee, so I had bought a package of coffee at the PX (Post Exchange). At that time, "real" coffee was not available in Germany except at high prices on the black market.

Following the police officer's directions, I rang the bell at Aunt Dora's apartment house a short while later. A woman whom I did not know opened the door. She was extremely surprised to find an American. I introduced myself and was immediately asked to enter the apartment. The woman was Aunt Dora's sister. She sadly told me that Aunt Dora had passed away several weeks before. However, the sister (whose name I have long forgotten) had been informed about my stamp album and the books I had left more than six years earlier.

The sister apologized that my books had been lost during an air raid. The stamp album, on the other hand, had survived the war. It had been given (by Aunt Dora) to my cousin Fanny Miloslawsky (later called Fay Miles). Fanny had survived incarceration at the Theresienstadt concentration camp and had returned to Berlin before immigrating to New York in 1946. (Aunt Dora's sister happily accepted my coffee.)

In the chapter "Why?" I discuss the terrible

miscalculation of the Jews living in Germany regarding the ultimate outcome of their fate. Now I have talked about Aunt Dora's pleas to my parents to leave the country, the sooner the better. She had understood the situation better than most Jews had. A case in point is my cousin by marriage, Eugen Miloslawsky, Fanny's husband.

Several days before my parents and I left Germany we briefly met with Fanny and Eugen to say goodbye. Eugen wished us well and mentioned that he was very happy to see us leave Germany because that was certainly safer for us. Then he added, "Nothing will happen to me because I am a disabled combat veteran of the German Army and also the recipient of the Iron Cross." (He had lost his left arm during World War I.) I am absolutely convinced that he really believed his statement. Eugen was first deported to Theresienstadt, and in 1944 to Auschwitz where he perished.

After my Army service, I returned to the U.S. in April 1948. At that time, I met my cousin Fanny. At our first reunion I received the stamp album. It is now in the possession of my daughter Monica. The album is without any monetary value, but it is a potent sign of friendship and courage by Aunt Dora, an exceptional German woman whom I loved. Unfortunately, there were not many more people like her.

This exemplary behavior of "Tante Dora" was the complete opposite from the behavior of another set of "friends." During the 1920s, my father's sister and brother-in-law had become extremely close with a German movie actor and producer named Paul Heidemann, and with his wife Betty. (Heidemann, an early German film pioneer, was usually seen in comic roles. He also directed and produced a number of films. Born in Cologne in 1884, he died in Berlin in 1968. His last film was produced around 1961.) The friendship with my relatives extended also to my parents and to me. My father became a *Duzfreund* of Paul Heidemann, i.e. they addressed each other by their first names and used the familiar *Du* instead of the formal *Sie* when speaking to each other. I addressed the Heidemanns as Uncle Paul and Aunt Betty.

The Heidemanns lived in a beautiful villa in the western part of the city, right at the Wannsee (one of the lakes surrounding Berlin). My favorite remembrance of that time was a ride in their motorboat. Uncle Paul allowed me to steer the boat for a while. What a thrill! There was a tremendous economic difference between the Heidemanns and my parents, but Uncle Paul and Aunt Betty never let me feel the gulf. I was invited to their only daughter's birthdays, the last time in the summer of 1934. Then, they suddenly broke off all contact with any part of my family. They might have contacted Ernst and Fanny Kleinmann to advise them that they could no longer associate with Jews. Given the situation at that time, I have my doubts that they would have been that "courteous." (By then the German film industry had become *judenrein*.) While Paul Heidemann became active again in the film industry after World War II there was never again any contact with my family.

The information Frau Dora Doss had relayed to my parents around 10:00 in the morning on November 10 was indeed based on facts. A teletype had been distributed to all central police stations shortly before midnight on November 9 by the then-head of the Gestapo, Hermann Müller. It advised the police of two important points: (1) "If" any "actions" (*Aktionen*) occur against Jews, their synagogues or property, the people involved in these acts are not to be hindered (*sie sollen nicht behindert werden*). (2) The arrest of 20–30,000 Jews is to be prepared; especially rich Jews are to be selected (*vor allem sind reiche Juden auszuwählen*). The reason rich Jews were to be arrested is obvious. In some cases, they were able to "buy" themselves out of concentration camps by "voluntarily" ceding their remaining property to the State.

Here my father's economic status might have helped. He certainly was not a "rich Jew" by any consideration. A Nazi regulation of April 26, 1938 had ordered the compulsory registration of all bank and brokerage accounts in excess of 5,000 marks that were held by Jews. He had nothing to register. Therefore, no Gestapo or police official looked for him. However, several acquaintances of my parents' were arrested and spent some time in concentration camps.

A day or two later we also received word of what had happened to my mother's younger brother Shlomo Bäcker (Uncle Salo to me). This uncle had a tailor shop in the western part of Berlin. In the back of the shop was a small but comfortable apartment that he shared with his wife and only daughter. In the early morning hours of November 10, several men, wearing civilian clothes, broke the windows of his store. He awakened and ran into the street to find out what had happened. Seeing the perpetrators, he tried to chase them away. In turn, they beat him savagely before disappearing. His wife had to take him to the Jewish Hospital. On January 12, 1939, he died at the hospital because of the injuries suffered. He became the first and tragically not the only member of our family to be killed by the Nazis.

A few months before Crystal Night, Uncle Salo's daughter Marion (Miriam), an ardent Zionist, had been able to immigrate to Palestine. Her mother succeeded at the beginning of 1939 in illegally crossing the German-Dutch border. She lived in Holland for a short while with her sister Ilse who had left Germany at the beginning of the Hitler regime. Sensing that living so close to the German border was not safe enough, however, she continued her emigration before the beginning of the war by escaping to Bolivia. There she worked as a cook in a mining camp. Her sister Ilse eventually became a victim of the Holocaust. After the end of World War II my aunt was reunited with her then-married daughter in Palestine. Miriam's husband, Yehuda Weiss, became one of the first casualties in the Israeli War of Independence in 1948. Soldiers of the Syrian Army in northern Israel ambushed his group. He was killed and his body severely mutilated. In contrast to his father-in-law, whom he had never met, he died with a rifle in his hand—a free citizen in a newly established Israel.

On November 12, 1938, Hermann Göring convened a meeting with top officials of the Nazi Government to discuss the "aftermath" of Crystal Night. At that time, the "rules" for eliminating Jews from the German economy were established. As he left the meeting, he is said to have made the infamous statement "I would not wish to be a Jew in Germany."

Four or five days after my father had taken refuge with his older sister, he returned. Our home life resumed, but from then on until the day we left Germany two years and eight months later, it was no longer the same. These few days had destroyed whatever sense of security we might still have had. It changed our feelings and the way even my father looked at Germany. From then on, the possibility of being incarcerated in a concentration camp was never too far away. The unthinkable had happened! The war against the Jews had taken a new turn; it was the "Prelude to Destruction."[38]

In a radio address to the German nation on New Year's Eve, December 31, 1938, the Nazi propaganda minister, Dr. Joseph Goebbels, referred to 1938 as the

---

[38] Sir Martin Gilbert, *Kristallnacht: Prelude to Destruction.* Harper Collins, 2006.

"most successful year of the regime" because of the incorporation of Austria (in March 1938) into the German Reich. He did not refer at all to the November events. However, in an essay dated January 21, 1939, Goebbels referred to the increasing number of "hate messages" emanating from the USA since November 10, 1938, without mentioning one word regarding the significance of that date. He also complained about the "completely unbearable interference by the mostly Jewish opinion makers [in the U.S.] in our inner-German affairs."[39]

Among the last laws issued by the Nazi regime, I found a regulation published by the Ministry of Economics on February 16, 1945. It read in part "whenever it is impossible to transfer documents citing anti-Jewish activities, they are to be destroyed to prevent their falling into the hands of the enemy."

---

[39] Joseph Goebbels, *Die Zeit ohne Beispiel* (Time without Example). Zentralverlag der NSDAP, München, 1941.

U.S. Army order for my first visit to Berlin after the end of World War II (text also appears on pages 189–190)

ORIGINAL

HEADQUARTERS
7707 EUROPEAN COMMAND INTELLIGENCE CENTER
APO 757   US ARMY

7 November 1947

SUBJECT: Leave Orders.

TO   : T/5 Bernard H. Burton, RA42242306, 7707 ECIC, APO 757, US Army.

   1. Under the provisions of Cir 57 EUCOM, dated 27 July 1947, Cir 9 EUCOM, dated 2 April 1947, as amended, and AR 600-115, the above named individual is hereby granted a leave of __three (3)__ days, effective on or about __13 November 1947__ for the purpose of visiting _____ __Berlin, Germany__

   2. The above named individual has sufficient funds to defray all anticipated expense incident to travel. No per diem nor reimbursement authorized for transportation costs advanced by this individual.

   3. Travel by Government aircraft is authorized on a space available basis. Facilities of ATC and EATS, such as messing, billeting and motor transportation will not be made available to this individual except at emergency stops due to weather or mechanical failure of the aircraft.

   4. Class IV priority, as defined in Sec IV, Cir 83, Hq USFET, dated 5 June 1946, is authorized, but in no event will official duty personnel be displaced by this individual.

   5. Outside the occupied zones, US Army messing, billeting and other facilities are not authorized and will not be provided and, further, the bearer of this document will not request any commander to provide such.

   6. Within the occupied zones, US Army messing, billeting and other facilities will be provided only after prior individual arrangements have been made and then only at the discretion of the commander concerned.

BY ORDER OF COLONEL THOROUGHMAN:

ROBERT A DORAN
1st Lt   AGD
Adjutant

DISTRIBUTION:
3-Individual concerned.
1-Headquarters Company
1-Adjutant (file)
1-Hq Comd

86

Back in Berlin in 1947

10

What Did We Eat?

A QUESTION RAISED by my friend Harry concerned the quantity and quality of food Jews were permitted to buy.

From the beginning of its existence, Nazi Germany pursued a policy of *Autarkie* (autarky), or economic self-sufficiency. The country was trying to become independent from foreign imports. The German word *Ersatz* (substitute), which eventually was taken over into other languages, became fashionable at that time. The Germans tried to produce a variety of imported items using German substitutes, not always successfully. In addition, from 1933 on, there were occasional shortages in imported fruit, butter, coffee, and other items. The entire population shared these shortages. Until March 11, 1940, Berlin's Jews could buy food along with all other inhabitants. I am not qualified to discuss this matter for Jews who lived outside of Berlin.

Before I go into further details regarding the food situation and its effect on Jews, I should relate a somewhat amusing food-related experience I had in early 1933.

Victor Klemperer's diaries about life under Hitler were published posthumously.[40] Under the date of March

---

[40] Victor Klemperer, *Tagebücher 1933–1941*. Berlin: Aufbau-Verlag, 1995.

22, 1933, he reported buying a tube of toothpaste with a swastika. While I personally have never seen such a tube, I have no doubt at all about the truthfulness of his statement.

His diary entry, however, reminded me of a somewhat different experience around that same time. Shortly after the Nazis came to power, a candy store in the neighborhood of our apartment began to sell *Hakenkreuzbonbons* (swastika candy). That candy was slightly larger and thicker than a Life Saver. The outside was red, the inside (instead of the hole) was white, and a black swastika was imprinted through the white. It had a sour taste and—much to the disgust of my mother— it became my favorite hard candy. I recollect that the swastika candy (and most probably also the toothpaste) was later prohibited by the Nazis, however, because it "denigrated" the swastika symbol.

In my review of Nazi laws applicable to Jews, I found an early order dated August 22, 1935. It stated specifically that sales of any merchandise to Jews should not be prohibited under any circumstances.[41] The quality and/or quantity bought by any consumer was dependent

---

[41] In a subsequent chapter "No German Social Security for Me," I have detailed some of the efforts by the Nazi regime to remove Jews as productive members of the German economy. On the other hand the Nazis were concerned (in the government's early years) about the effect of a reduction of consumption by Jews, which might become a detriment to the economy as a whole; hence the above-mentioned edict of August 1935. To show, however, the extent of their wide-ranging instructions I add two related ordinances. Savings banks were advised on September 11, 1935 not to boycott Jewish deposits and not to close Jewish accounts. (This obviously made it easier to control Jewish wealth and be prepared for subsequent confiscation.) On June 14, 1938, the Ministry of Economics reiterated that it was the policy of the government to exclude Jews rapidly from the economy. Loans and credits to Jewish people and to their businesses were no longer to be extended! However, the Ministry repeated that it was not desirable to refuse bank deposits from Jews.

strictly on availability and price. The only exception as far as observant Jews were concerned was the fact that beginning in 1933 kosher meat became generally unavailable. The first regulations prohibiting kosher meat varied according to the German states. An order dated March 22, 1933 prohibited ritual slaughtering in Saxony. Another order of April 4, 1933 prohibited the importation of kosher meat into Baden. Finally on April 21, 1933 kosher slaughtering was prohibited for all of Germany. Strangely, however, Hermann Göring, in his capacity as the Prussian Minister President, permitted the importation of kosher meat (order dated August 18, 1933). The latter permission, possibly issued for foreign policy reasons, became somewhat meaningless. Imported kosher meat had to be paid for in foreign currency. However, the appropriate German banking institutions would not, in many cases, permit such "extravagant" use of scarce foreign resources.

My parents did not keep a kosher home so these regulations did not inconvenience me personally. My mother's older sister, however, was extremely upset by this drastic change. I vaguely recall that some rabbis in Berlin supposedly permitted their congregations to buy non-kosher meat (except for pork, of course) which at that time was euphemistically called *neu-koscher* (new kosher).

During the last week in August 1939, Germany began to issue rationing cards to all inhabitants. In my letter to Harry Pomeranz written from Cuba in late 1941, I mentioned that "at the beginning" the amount of food allocated to Jews and Aryans was the same. The cards allowed the distribution of items for four categories: (1) unrationed items, (2) basic rations for normal consumers, (3) supplementary rations for workers doing heavy manual labor (*Schwerarbeiter*), pregnant or nursing women and (4) occasional extra allotments of rationed food.

The initial *weekly* allowances included about 300 grams (10½ oz) of fats and/or oil and 700 grams (24½ oz) of meat and meat products. At that time, Jews were also entitled to 63 grams (2.2 oz) of coffee substitutes and 20 grams (.7 oz) of tea. That did not last too long. As early as December 1, 1939 the regional ration and distribution offices were instructed to deprive Jews of special food allocations for the period starting December 18, 1939. From then on Jews received less meat, less fat, no cocoa and no rice. These instructions were not permitted to be published in the German press.

The secret police had advised its offices on September 12, 1939 to conduct searches in Jewish apartments for *Hamsterwaren* (items hoarded and/or bought on the black market). The police notice also stated that any such items found are to be confiscated and the owner taken into *Schutzhaft* (literally, preventive detention), a "legal" term used by the Nazis denoting incarceration in a concentration camp.

On March 11, 1940, a new order required all ration coupons distributed to Jews to be stamped with a "J" (*Jude*). At the same time the local authorities were "granted the right" to set aside shopping hours for Jews. Officially, the shopping hours were restricted so as not to "inconvenience" Aryan shoppers. In Berlin, the established "shopping hour" for Jews was set between four and five PM. In effect, this meant that any item sold on a first-come-first-served basis did not become available for Jews at all. Other areas of Germany had different arrangements. However, the general restrictions curtailing access for Jews to non-rationed goods and limiting the time for purchases prevailed.

By the time I left Germany, the weekly food allowances for Jews included 125 grams (4.375 oz) of fat and 400 grams (14 oz) of meat or meat products. Aryans were entitled to additional monthly allotments of chicken and fish—nothing for Jews. In my letter to Harry I described the allotment of bread and sugar as "sufficient." Yet, I do not remember what I might have meant by the use of that word. Fruit was generally not available for Jews and chocolate and other sweets were allocated to Aryan children only. Around July 1940, our neighbor's son—who had been drafted into the German Army—returned on leave from German-occupied France. He arrived with, among other loot, several bars of Cadbury chocolate. His mother, who remained a "good" neighbor to my family throughout the Hitler years, gave one to me. That was the only time between August 1939 and July 1941, when I had left Germany, that I tasted chocolate.

In spite of the lower food allowances, I should say, however, that I have no recollection of actually ever having been hungry. I cannot tell with any degree of accuracy whether this meant that the food we were permitted to buy was sufficient or to what extent my mother may have given me a "disproportional" amount of the family's allotment.

On May 13, 1945, or about five days after Germany's unconditional surrender, the Berlin municipal authorities published an order of the resident military commander, (Soviet) Lt. Gen. Bersarin, detailing the distribution of food to the population. Depending upon the type of work performed, similar to the distribution pattern established in 1939, the initial post-war rations for Berliners were set at between 280 and 700 grams (9.8–24.5 oz) of meat and 70–210 grams (2.45–5.825 oz) of fat. There were also allowances for "real" coffee, coffee substitutes and tea, as well as rations for bread (2800–4200 grams, or 98–147 oz), sugar (105–175 grams, or 3.675–6.125 oz) and potatoes (2800 grams, or 98 oz), all on a weekly basis.

In other words, after an extremely bitter war, Berliners received larger food rations from their erstwhile enemy than the Nazis had allotted to Jews in 1941 and subsequent years.[42]

---

[42] I have extracted the information about the initial food allowances after the end of the war from a pamphlet, *An die Bevölkerung der Stadt Berlin* (To the Inhabitants of the City of Berlin), published by the Berlin City Administration on May 13, 1945. I obtained this paper in late 2003 after the death of my friend Hannelore Shelton, when I found it among her belongings. Hannelore was a former fellow student of the *Mittelschule* who survived the war years in Berlin. She had brought the paper with her when she emigrated to the U.S. in 1946.

11

No German Social Security for Me

IN A PREVIOUS chapter, "The Jewish Hospital in Berlin and My First Encounter with Women's Equality," I discussed my correspondence with Dr. Anne Lerner. I had mentioned to her in a letter that "a great deal of luck" was one of the factors in the survival of some of my friends, as well as of my parents and me. We may call it that or "God's will;" we may use the Yiddish word *bashert* (pre-ordained) or other similar expressions; no matter what term we use, it is apparent that my parents and I were extremely fortunate in being able to leave Germany with practically the last train.

In his letter to me, Harry Pomeranz questioned another aspect of the ever-worsening situation of the Jews in Germany before they were dispatched to the "final solution." A part of the very first question he raised was "Is it true that all Jews were required to engage in compulsory labor service?"

The Nazi regime started by slowly—and then ever faster—eliminating Jews from their normal employment and from having any contact with the general population. The *initial* anti-Jewish work laws, as bitter as they may have been, were directed until November 1938 "only" at specific professions. Not all Jews were affected! This may have given many of them a false sense of security—until it was too late. Some random examples taken from laws and regulations between 1933 and 1941 will suffice.

An early Nazi regulation, dated March 31, 1933 included the following statement: "Jewish judges and other Jewish jurists working at courthouses are to be summarily relieved of their duties. They are prohibited from entering the courthouses." All Jewish teachers at city-owned schools in Berlin were equally relieved of their duties as of April 1, 1933. A law of June 30, 1933 required the dismissal of all Jewish officials and of those Aryan officials who were married to "non-Aryans."

On July 3, 1933, the Berlin stock exchange cancelled the approbation for *all* brokers effective September 30. At the same time, it announced that new broker licenses would be issued to people who are "honorable and trustworthy." This was the "polite" explanation for forcing Jews out of that business.

On July 29, 1933, the Commissioner for Medical Affairs prohibited any "ethnic German physician" from consulting with any physician of a "foreign race," and prohibited two such physicians from taking each other's place.

In March 1935 an order of the Reich Chamber for Literature (*Reichsschrifttumskammer*) required all Jewish writers, poets, editors, publicists, etc. to cease any writing or other literary activity while in Germany.[43] Around the same time, Jews were prohibited from working in the advertising industry or as store window decorators.

---

[43] An order of April 24, 1935 required all newspaper publishers to submit their "pure Aryan background" going as far back as the year 1800! This regulation had the strange title "Order for the Preservation of Independence of the Press" (*Anordnung zur Wahrung der Unabhängigkeit des Zeitungswesens*). The title was supposed to indicate the independence of the press, which in reality had not been independent since 1933.

Effective May 5, 1935 Jews could no longer serve as expert witnesses in judicial proceedings. On October 17, 1935, all Jewish movie house owners were ordered to "sell" their business no later than December 12 of the same year. All Jewish-owned employment agencies were closed November 5, 1935. Finally, the few remaining Jewish officials of whatever capacity who might have still been working in national or local government had to resign their positions by December 31, 1935.

Jewish CPAs were advised on November 5, 1938 to cease their operations as of December 31, 1938. On December 11, 1938, an elaborate law was published under the title "Order to Exclude Jews from the German Economy" (*Anordnung zur Ausschaltung der Juden aus der deutschen Wirtschaft*). Under that law, Jews were prohibited from owning or managing retail or mail order stores or offices or to practice any trade. They could not be active in any managerial position of any business organization. Additionally, they were prohibited from receiving any unemployment or other contractual insurance or other compensation for the loss of their employment.

On December 23, 1938, the city of Berlin issued an edict prohibiting Jews from entering any unemployment office. From then on, a newly formed "Central Labor Office for Jews" was responsible for Berlin's unemployed Jews, who were increasingly being recruited as laborers on construction projects and in repairing railroad tracks; these were jobs most of them were ill-suited to handle, and that paid minimum wages.[44]

---

[44] The Ministry of Labor complained in November 1939 that the percentage of Jews excused from participating in heavy manual labor on account of physical disabilities was too high. It therefore required that those Jews be reexamined (*Die Juden sind deshalb auf ihre Einsatzfähigkeit für körperliche Arbeiten erneut zu überprüfen*).

This situation continued until a new law was issued on March 3, 1941: "Obligation to Work for all Jews above the Age of 14 Years" (*Arbeitsverpflichtung aller Juden über 14 Jahre*). My answer to Harry's initial question was obvious. By 1941, all Jews still living in Germany were obligated to work—but in almost all cases, not in their professions. (There were no Jews that I knew who were experts in laying railroad tracks.)

The new obligation to work was an extremely serious matter for the very few people like my parents and me who were still actively trying to leave Germany. Most Jews no longer had any chance to leave. There were rumors that Jews who were conscripted to work could no longer emigrate because of their "importance" to the German war effort.

It is difficult to assess—at the beginning of the twenty-first century—what was then a rumor and what was the truth. Yet, I do remember that my family was lucky in not being drafted for any work project for Jews during the March to July 1941 period we spent in Germany. My mother came closest. In May or June, she received a letter requiring her appearance at the Jewish Labor Office in order to enlist for work. Luckily, Mr. Siegfried Zadek, a minor functionary of the Jewish Community Service in Berlin (and the father of my girlfriend), was able to use his influence to obtain a delay for my mother, and she was "temporarily excused."[45]

---

[45] Mr. Siegfried Zadek helped us and quite possibly saved our lives, but unfortunately he was not able to help himself or his family. The Zadeks were deported in one of the early transports on April 2, 1942 and sent to a "labor camp" in Trawniki (District of Lublin, Poland) together with some 1,713 people, mostly from Berlin. My mother's oldest brother and his wife were also in that group. All of them perished. The Trawniki camp, established in the fall of 1941, was part of a network of similar extermination camps organized by an SS officer, Globocnik. It is not

97

I was equally fortunate. After graduation from the Middle High School, I attended a School for Languages, maintained by the Jewish Community in Berlin. At that school, I took lessons in English and Spanish, including shorthand in those languages, and bookkeeping. On May 16 and 17, 1941, all girls in my class were ordered to report to work at a factory. Purely by mistake, the three boys in the class (I among them) did not receive any such orders. The director of the school, realizing what had happened, placed us three in the few still-existing adult classes. Consequently, I continued to attend the Language School until a few days before my emigration.

Therefore, I am happy not to have any right to German social security, as I never worked in that country. If I had, it might have cost me my life.

I have no exact recollection what most of my fellow graduates from the Middle School were doing at that time. Irving Klothen, together with another boy, continued his academic studies by transferring to the Jewish Gymnasium (high school). Jerry Bocian went to an agricultural camp and I believe the other boys must have worked in required factory assignments. The four girls attended a still-existing Jewish school for nannies.

At the beginning of this chapter, I referred to the chilling phrase "final solution." An explanation regarding these two disturbing words is in order.

Very simplistically speaking, there are several events which "logically" follow each other and culminated in setting the stage for the eventual killing of some six million Jews.

At first, Adolf Hitler "explained" his war against the Jews in semi-religious terms. In his book *Mein Kampf* (My

---

quite clear whether Globocnik was killed in May 1944 or committed suicide in June 1945.

Battle), written around the mid 1920s, he stated "I believe that I act in accordance with the requirements of the Almighty Creator: By defending myself against the Jew, I fight for the work of the Lord." (*So glaube ich heute im Sinne des almächtigen Schöpfers zu handeln: Indem ich mich des Juden erwehre, kämpfe ich für das Werk des Herrn.*)[46] However, later in the same book he is more direct, stating that Germany can only be liberated by removing the foreign bacillus (*Erreger*)[47] from her. There is no doubt throughout his writings who was considered by him to be this foreign agent. There are numerous other statements in *Mein Kampf* relating to the eventual destruction of the Jewish "race."

Strengthening this thought is a *New York Times* article of April 22, 2004. It reported a previously unpublicized diary by James G. McDonald, a U.S. diplomat who was the League of Nations high commissioner for refugees (and later the first U.S. ambassador to Israel). The diary, now in the possession of the U.S. Holocaust Memorial Museum, shows that "Mr. McDonald believed as early as 1933 that the Nazis were considering the mass killing of Europe's Jews."[48] In my opinion, he had correctly assessed the situation. I obviously do not know whether McDonald had read *Mein Kampf.* He mentioned, however, that he had met Hitler personally.

On December 8, 1931, i.e. more than a year before Hitler assumed power, the German government issued an emergency decree (*Notverordnung*) for the "protection of the economy." One of the main points in this new law was the attempt to prevent the flight of capital by establishing a

---

[46] Adolf Hitler, *Mein Kampf* (My Battle). Munich: Zentralverlag der NSDAP, 1941, p. 70.
[47] Ibid p. 372.
[48] *The New York Times*, "Nazis and Jews: Insights from Old Diary," by Neil A. Lewis, p. A3.

so-called *Reichsfluchtsteuer* (Reich escape tax). I am not an economist but I believe that this "temporary" law may have been reasonable under the then-existing economic circumstances. In the first year of its existence (pre-Hitler), it was an attempt to tax, at the rate of twenty-five percent, relatively "rich people"—those with assets in excess of 200,000 marks (at that time approximately $50,000)—who *voluntarily* were leaving Germany.

With the onset of the Nazi regime, this emergency regulation, however, continued to be the law. When starting to force Jews out of Germany, it became a most important cog in the Nazi policy to reduce substantially the ability of Jews to emigrate with their assets. On July 26, 1933, six months after the Nazis assumed power, the Finance Ministry issued a declaration stating that the emigration of Jews was desirable, and therefore must not be prevented. The declaration continued that emigration of "solvent" people (those able to pay) decreases the tax basis for Germany and therefore a "last big contribution" is to be levied. The calculation of this "contribution" was based upon the prior (pre-Hitler) temporary emergency law as "modified" by the Nazis. After all, at this point the Jews. who were leaving Germany did so under extreme pressure by the government. This was not, by any means, a voluntary maneuver, as contemplated in the original law. In the last two and a half years in which emigration was still possible (1939 to 1941), the tax went from one hundred percent for emigrants from Berlin to about five hundred percent for Jews leaving some southern German cities.[49] I have no explanation for the enormous differential in the rates. It appears that some local authorities simply added certain percentages to increase the "last big contribution."

---

[49] See also Moshe Ayalon's "Report on the living conditions of the Jews in Germany." Published by the Leo Baeck Institute, Year Book 1998 (Secker & Warburg, London), pages 271–285.

October 1934 saw the "adaptation of the German tax code" (*Steueranpassungsgesetz*). This meant that from then on all existing tax laws and all facts in potential tax cases had to be interpreted in accordance with the Nazi point of view. With this "simple" step, the Nazi ideology had become the decisive proviso for all taxation decisions. Consequently, this law saved laborious changes to individual tax laws and decrees. (Examples: If a Jew sued a non-Jew, the former had to be wrong. If the government accused a Jew of tax fraud, the government was correct.)

Most importantly, arbitrariness, i.e. discrimination against people "outside" of the German community (say, Jews) had now become legal. Consequently, Jews could be "legally" deprived of their rights, and their material wealth reduced or confiscated, since the judiciary effectively adopted this ideology for all other proceedings.

In the "Letter to my Grandchildren" I mentioned the establishment, on January 24, 1939, of a special central office to "speed up" emigration. Referring to that "office assignment" Hermann Göring wrote a letter, dated July 31, 1941, to the then-chief of the Security Police, Reinhard Heydrich, requesting that the latter take all necessary steps to prepare a "total solution" (*Gesamtlösung*) of the "Jewish question" in the German sphere of influence in Europe. That letter, incidentally, was written within ten days after my parents and I had crossed the French-Spanish border. As I previously stated, emigration of Jews from Germany was prohibited as of October 27, 1941, and with Hitler's approval, "evacuation" to the East (occupied Poland) was ordered.

The Göring-to-Heydrich letter was acted upon at the ill-famed "Wannsee Conference" of January 20, 1942, which addressed the "Final Solution" (*Endlösung*) and discussed in detail how Jews deported from western to eastern Europe should first be employed as forced laborers, and then eventually killed.[50] The conference protocol listed over eleven million Jews to be eliminated, including five million from the Soviet Union and even 330,000 from England. There were no Jews to be killed in Estonia. That country was by then considered already *judenfrei* (free of Jews).

As if to underscore his hatred for the Jews and his coming plans, Hitler had declared in a major speech before the Reichstag (Parliament) on January 30, 1939, "If the international Jewish financiers in and outside Europe should succeed in plunging the nations once more into a world war, then the result will not be the victory of Jewry, but the annihilation of the Jewish race in Europe!" (*Wenn es den internationalen Finanzjuden in und ausserhalb Europas gelingen sollte die Völker noch einmal in einen Weltkrieg zu stürzen, dann wird das Ergebnis nicht der Sieg des Juden sein, sondern die Vernichtung der jüdischen Rasse in Europa.)*[51] Hitler made this threat in only *19 seconds*. Yet, he substantially carried it out within the following six years. While I distinctly remember hearing that speech at our neighbor's apartment (we had no radio), I do not remember my reaction at that time, nor did I understand the seriousness of his statement. Most probably, I must have been "relieved" that Hitler "only" made threats and did not announce any new, immediate anti-Jewish actions or decrees.

Hitler's fanatical hatred of Jews never changed! The *last* paragraph of his Testament, which he signed on April 29, 1945, one day before he committed suicide, stated, "Above all I call upon the leadership of the nation and

---

[50] *Das Wannsee-Protokoll zur Endlösung der Judenfrage.* (Wannsee-Protocol for the Final Solution of the Jewish Question), published by the Informationszentrum Berlin, Stauffenbergstrasse, Berlin.
[51] See also "Hear Hitler Speak in German,"
www.historyplace.com/worldwar2/timeline/threat.htm.

those who follow it to scrupulous observance of the racial laws and to fight mercilessly against the poisoners of all the peoples of the world, the international Jewry."[52]

[52] Quoted by Richard von Weizsäcker, President of Germany, in his speech to the German Parliament on May 8, 1985, entitled "On the fortieth anniversary of the end of the war in Europe and the national socialist tyranny."

12

Trying to Emigrate

IN SPITE OF everything I have written about my father's great reluctance to leave Germany, I do not want to leave anyone with the mistaken impression that no attempts to emigrate were made during the earlier years of the Hitler regime.

Around December 1932, my aunt and uncle left on their annual winter vacation. Contrary to their usual trip to St. Moritz in Switzerland (which they had visited for about the last ten seasons), they opted for a cruise on the Mediterranean and traveled extensively through Palestine and Egypt. At the beginning of February 1933, they returned to a different Germany than the one they had left not too long before. While they were abroad on vacation, Hitler had become Chancellor of Germany.

Within days of their return my aunt visited us. She spoke enthusiastically of the thriving Jewish community in Palestine. Suddenly she had become a Zionist. While her main topic concerned the altered political situation in Germany, she mentioned that the Ruthenberg Electricity Works would employ my father immediately upon arrival in Palestine, since trained electricians were in short supply. She also suggested that my uncle was acquainted with some members of the company's management.

Her presentation included another sweetener. At that time, Great Britain was the mandatory power in

Palestine and strict regulations were enforced to hold immigration of newcomers to an absolute minimum. To make it easier and to help us, my uncle had promised to transfer 1,000 British pounds, a fortune at that time, to allow our family to immigrate as "capitalists," outside the restrictive regulations.

If Papa had accepted that generous proposal, we would have been able to leave Germany literally within a few weeks. Papa, however, declined, using the explanation which was then current among Jews in Germany: "Things will not become that bad!" (*Es wird schon nicht so schlimm werden!*) He was obviously wrong (and so were more than 500,000 other Jews). Nevertheless, there went the first opportunity to leave Germany.

I must give my aunt credit. She had not been able to convince her brother to leave. Therefore, for the next year or so she concentrated on getting *me* out of Germany. There was an international school near Lago di Garda (Lake Garda) in northern Italy. I have long forgotten the school's name. Applications were sent out but for reasons I had never been told, I was not accepted.

She then arranged for another application, this time to the Mikve Israel Agricultural School in Palestine, a school established in 1870 which is still in existence at the time I am writing these remembrances. I was about 11 or 12 years old and had never shown any interest in agriculture. However, for my aunt it meant another possibility to get at least her only nephew out of Germany. Again, for reasons unknown, I was not accepted. While I was not a top scholar in middle school at that time, I believe my grades were reasonably good. My aunt had also guaranteed the payment of tuition and living expenses. Therefore, the non-acceptance (of both school applications) must have been based on other grounds.

Before continuing to describe further attempts to emigrate, I should mention that my uncle and aunt had left Germany for the last time in early 1934. They continued to retain their beautiful apartment in Berlin. It was confiscated at the beginning of the war when it became clear to the authorities that they would not return to Germany. Initially they settled in France, staying at the Hotel Plaza Athenée in Paris from 1934 to early 1939. They then boarded the SS Normandie,[53] went to the U.S. and shortly thereafter bought a house in southern California.[54] Contrary to other immigrants, they did not need an affidavit of support. My uncle had seen to it that whatever liquid assets he had been able to get out of Germany since before 1933 were by then located in the U.S.

With the only relatives my parents had to assist with our emigration now in France, all requests and instructions came first from France and later the U.S. In spite of the distance, my aunt had not given up; she continued her search for a safe haven for us.

I recall there were serious attempts between 1935 and 1937 to immigrate to Australia and to Brazil. In both cases, I remember seeing voluminous application papers

[53] Launched in 1932, the SS *Normandie* was at that time the largest and fastest ship in the world. In 1942, while being converted to a troopship during WWII, the *Normandie* caught fire, capsized and sank at pier 88 in New York.

[54] They became part of the German-speaking community that existed from 1939 on the west coast, the "Weimar on the Pacific." Many of the German intellectuals and known film directors and actors settled in that area. Ernst Lubitsch, the noted film director, had been a neighbor of theirs in their apartment house in Berlin in the 1920s. The actor Felix Bressart, well-known in pre-Hitler Germany, also worked in Hollywood albeit in smaller roles (in *Ninotchka* with Greta Garbo and in *To Be or Not to Be* with Jack Benny). He built his villa in the same style after seeing the house my aunt and uncle had bought. Occasionally they also had contacts with the German writers Lion Feuchtwanger and Heinrich Mann, all acquaintances from the "old country." (See also "When Weimar Luminaries Went West Coast," in the travel section of the *New York Times*, October 5, 2008.)

that were sent to those countries. After months of waiting the only developments were rejection letters.

When visiting the Melbourne Immigration Museum in November 2008, my eyes were drawn to a sign reading as follows: "More than nine million people have migrated to Australia since 1788. Countless others have tried and failed." It was only at that visit that I became fully aware of the restrictive immigration laws that prevailed in the Commonwealth of Australia during the time my parents tried to find a refuge.

The Australian Immigration Restriction Act was in effect from 1901 to 1945. In 1938, however, the Australian government announced that it would permit the entry of 15,000 Jewish and non-Jewish refugees from Nazism. With the onset of the war, however, German Jews became "enemy aliens" who were then denied permission to enter Australia.

My family's last major pre-war goal was Great Britain, which at that time had opened its gates to allow Jewish children to find refuge, by way of the so-called *Kindertransport*,[55] and it accepted young Jewish males. My aunt was successful in obtaining residence visas for the three of us. Those papers arrived in August 1939. Before taking advantage of this possibility, I had to obtain a passport in my own name. I have no knowledge of why my parents had not applied for my passport any earlier. It is probable that by that time the German authorities would only act upon a passport application if you were in direct need of such a document. Whatever the reasons, I finally received a passport in my own name, on August 25, 1939.

---

[55] Starting in November/December 1938, the Central British Fund for German Jewry in Great Britain lobbied the government and raised funds to get Jewish children out of Germany (which included, at that point, Austria and Czechoslovakia). This rescue of approximately 10,000 children became known as the *Kindertransport* (children's transport).

That same day my parents and I went to the British consulate and were told that the Visa Department had been closed either that day or the day before. The consular official with whom we talked suggested we leave Germany immediately by illegally crossing either the Belgian or Dutch borders and presenting ourselves at one of the British consulates in those countries. We would then receive our British visas. My parents were afraid to contemplate such a most dangerous trip. They were right in this instance. I cannot believe that at this late stage we would have been able to cross any border illegally. German troops marched into Poland only seven days later and started World War II.

13

Why?

THESE REMEMBRANCES COVER events that occurred more than 60-odd years ago. Yet, to this day, I have the greatest difficulty in coming to terms with my father's reaction to the onset of the Hitler regime. Because of our family's connections and pleading (and also the great love and respect he had for his sister and the assistance offered by her and his brother-in-law), we should have been among the first instead of the last ones to escape the Nazis. Although my father was born in Germany, most of his relatives and his Jewish friends were "foreign-born." He could not have had the same love and affection for Germany as many (most?) of the "German" Jews. If it had been solely up to my mother, I believe we might have emigrated earlier. It should also be noted that with one single exception *all* of my parents' non-Jewish "friends" had stopped seeing us by about 1934. That great exception, Aunt Dora, I have mentioned in a previous chapter.[56]

Everything I have read and everything I have

---

[56] The early loss of non-Jewish friends was not a phenomenon unique to my parents. In an essay about the German-born American political theorist Hannah Arendt, the respected German historian and journalist Joachim Fest quoted her as having stated, "...yesterday we still received telephone calls, letters, and visits from all over. Suddenly silence descended"(Joachim Fest. *Der Spiegel.* September 13, 2004). Hannah Arendt was arrested for doing research on anti-Semitic propaganda, and on her release fled Germany for France. She arrived in the U.S. in 1941.

written in the foregoing pages clearly pointed to the eventual destruction of the Jews remaining in Germany. I am not even touching upon the much broader "final solution" regarding all European Jews. From a purely personal point of view, it is exhilarating that my parents and I escaped the most degrading and deadly years of the Hitler era. The tragic part is that my father was not alone in misjudging the horrible consequences. The Nazis killed more than 160,000 Jews who lived in Germany;[57] they are the "silenced" witnesses to this "miscalculation." Why this terrible misjudgment?

This "Why?" is perhaps the most important question that has been with me for many years. Why did so many Jews in Germany not recognize the literal handwriting on the wall until it was too late?

More than a year after Hitler assumed power, a Jewish Encyclopedia was published in Berlin.[58] In explaining the word "emancipation," it starts correctly with the freedom of religion guaranteed by the Virginia Declaration of Rights in 1776.[59] It mentions the French Assembly in 1790 that declared equal rights for Jews, and the Prussian edict of March 11, 1812 that recognized Jews as Prussian nationals.[60]

---

[57] The German *Bundesarchiv* (Federal Archives) issued a *Commemorative Book for the German Victims of the Holocaust* (*Gedenkbuch für die deutschen Opfer des Holocaust*). Its second edition lists 149,625 names. At the beginning of 1933, Germany had an estimated Jewish population of 509,000 (400,000 of them were German citizens), or .8% of the total population. About 380,000 other people were of "Jewish ancestry." Greater Berlin's Jewish population was about 150,000. At the time my parents and I left Germany, about 50,000 Jews remained in Berlin; practically all of them became victims of the Holocaust.

[58] *Philo-Lexikon*. Berlin: Philo Verlag und Buchhandlung GmbH, 1934.

[59] Section 16 of that Declaration states "... all men are equally entitled to the free exercise of religion."

[60] On that day, Prince Karl-August von Hardenberg signed the decree giving Jews the rights of Prussian nationals, *except for the right to*

The disturbing and tragic narration is at the end of the brief article, which explains that since 1933 (by virtue of the anti-Jewish laws that had been issued by the time the encyclopedia went to press) the emancipation of German Jews had been "restricted" (*eingeschränkt*). I believe that the word "restricted" with regard to the emancipation of German Jews was the feeling of the large majority of the Jews living in Germany at that time.

There were some exceptions to this belief. In a letter dated June 8, 1933, to the then-mayor of Tel Aviv, Meir Dizengoff, the German-Jewish artist, 85-year-old Max Liebermann, talked of the "revocation of equal rights" (*Aufhebung der Gleichberechtigung*).[61] However, by 1934/35 most other Jews in Germany had not yet realized the deadly purpose of the Nazi regime.

In further researching the earlier question (Why?) I came across an assessment by Raul Hilberg, one of the foremost historians of that era. His explanation may not satisfy everyone but it gave me a better insight. Hilberg also expressed this "Jewish" attitude to the oncoming destruction better than I could have stated it. Here are just a few quotations from his monumental three-volume study:[62]

---

become government officials or to serve as officers in the army or navy. Beginning with the Congress of Vienna in 1815, these rights of citizenship for Jews were restricted. This continued until 1866 when Jews were again granted citizenship, and in 1871 the citizenship was extended to all Jews of the newly founded German Empire.

[61] Quoted in a special edition of *Der Spiegel, Juden und Deutsche* (Jews and Germans), page 110. Hamburg: Spiegel Verlag Rudolf Augstein GmbH &Co. KG, August 1992. Max Liebermann (1847–1935) was a leading German impressionist and graphic artist. He served as president of the Prussian Academy of Arts from 1920 until his dismissal by the Nazis in 1933. Martha Liebermann, his widow, remained in Berlin after the death of her husband. At age 84, having been arrested by the Gestapo, she committed suicide in March 1943 before she could be transported to a death camp.

[62] Raul H. Hilberg, *The Destruction of the European Jews*. New York:

Since the fourth century after Christ there have been three anti-Jewish policies: conversion, expulsion and annihilation (page 8).

Preventative attack, armed resistance, and revenge were almost completely absent in Jewish exilic history. ... The Jews of Europe were placing themselves under the protection of constituted authority. This reliance was legal, physical and psychological (page 22).

... Alleviation attempts were typical and instantaneous responses by the Jewish community. Under the heading of alleviation are included petitions, protection payments, ransom arrangements, anticipatory compliance, relief, salvage, reconstruction—in short, all those activities designed to avert danger or, in the event that force has already been used, to diminish its efforts (page 23).

In the early 1920s, Hugo Bettauer[63] wrote a fantasy novel entitled *Die Stadt ohne Juden* (The City without Jews). This novel depicts an expulsion of the Jews from Vienna. The author shows how Vienna cannot get along without its Jews.

Holmes & Meier Publishers, Inc., 1985.
[63] Hugo Bettauer, *The City Without Jews*. New York: Bloch Publishing Company, 1926. In an introduction to the American edition, the translator Salomea Neumark Brainin explained that Hugo Bettauer was killed (in 1925) by a "Nordic" who believed that Bettauer was a menace to the German *Kultur* (culture). Bettauer, a native of Vienna, immigrated to the U.S. and became a U.S. citizen around the turn of the twentieth century. However, some ten years later he returned to his native Vienna and became the co-publisher of a weekly magazine devoted to "married love." The magazine was considered immoral by Viennese authorities. In a subsequent trial he was found innocent but his attitude and the fact that he was Jewish led to his murder in 1925.

Ultimately, the Jews are recalled. That was the mentality of Jewry, and Jewish leadership, on the eve of the destruction process. When the Nazis took over in 1933, the old Jewish reaction pattern set in again, but this time the results were catastrophic. The Jewish pleading did not slow the German bureaucracy; it was not stopped by Jewish indispensability. Without regard to cost,[64] the bureaucratic machines operating with accelerating speed and ever-widening destructive effect proceeded to annihilate European Jews. ... We see, therefore, that both perpetrators and victims draw upon their age-old experiences in dealing with each other. The Germans did it with success. The Jews did it with disaster (page 28).

Hitler and his movement treated anti-Semitism as the one element which was supposed to surmount all social and economic differences among their members. Hatred against the Jews was used to bring about the desired sense of a German community (*Volksgemeinschaft*).

In the opening paragraph of this chapter, I have wondered about my father's seeming disbelief of the ultimate goal of the Hitler regime with regard to the "Jewish Question." Yet, I have to make two important qualifications.

I am not at all sure—even at this late date—how I

---

[64] See also Sebastian Haffner, *The Meaning of Hitler*. New York: McMillan Publishing Co., Inc., 1979. In discussing the extermination of Jews during the war years, Haffner stated (on page 126) that these actions "impeded the conduct of the war because thousands of SS men, who were fit for active service, were lacking at the front—all in all the equivalent of several divisions—and because the daily mass transports to the extermination camps ... were depriving the fighting forces of an appreciable amount of rolling stock which was in short supply and which was urgently needed..."

would have reacted as an adult living in Germany in the years 1933 to say 1938. It is very easy, with 20/20 hindsight, to state that one should have seen what was coming. It is much harder when you actually lived during those times and—especially at the beginning—the anti-Jewish measures did not always affect you personally. They only pertained to "other Jews!" An example of the latter would be the April 7, 1933 Law for the Restoration of the Professional Civil Service. That law effectively excluded Jews (or "non-Aryans," as they were then called) from employment as instructors in all public educational institutions; as officials of public works, etc. or employees of other public or semi-public agencies; and as police officers and civil employees of the Army. Nowadays we can see a trend developing. Then it was not quite that clear.

The second point refers to a much later event. In late July 1942 a German industrialist, Eduard Schulte,[65] managing director of a mining company, learned of the secret so-called "Wannsee Protocol" of January 1942, previously discussed, which made it official German policy to exterminate Jews. Mr. Schulte to his everlasting credit transmitted his knowledge (via intermediaries) to a Berlin-born Jewish lawyer then living in Geneva, Switzerland. Dr. Gerhart Riegner was at that time an official of the World Jewish Congress. He reviewed the information given to him and on August 8, 1942 requested the U.S. Vice Consul in Geneva to transmit it to the State Department. He also

---

[65] Eduard Schulte was in contact with Allen Dulles of the (U.S.) Office of Strategic Services (which later became the Central Intelligence Agency). When Schulte was advised by German intelligence officials in December 1943 that the Gestapo was about to arrest him, he fled to Switzerland where, for the remainder of the war, he continued to work for Dulles. Schulte never publicly acknowledged his leaking of the Wannsee Protocol after the war had ended. He lived in Switzerland until his death in 1966. (For further information, see also U.S. Holocaust Memorial Museum, Holocaust Encyclopedia, Eduard Schulte.)

informed the local British consular officials and petitioned them to inform the British Foreign Office.

The first reaction of the U.S. State Department was to call the information sent by Riegner a fantastic war rumor. However, on December 17, 1942 the State Department issued a press release stating that the attention of the Allies' governments has been drawn to

> numerous reports from Europe that the German authorities ... are now carrying into effect Hitler's oft-repeated intention to exterminate the Jewish people in Europe. ... The number of victims of these bloody cruelties is reckoned in many hundreds of thousands of entirely innocent men, women and children. The (Allied) Governments condemn in the strongest possible terms this bestial policy of cold-blooded extermination. ... They reaffirm their solemn resolution to insure that those responsible for these crimes shall not escape retribution ...

Unfortunately, these and other "condemnations" had no effect on the ultimate outcome of the Holocaust. While the release by the State Department talks of "hundreds of thousands" of victims, it is estimated that in 1942 alone, 2.7 million Jews lost their lives—the most lethal year in Jewish history.[66]

There is no doubt in my mind that the earlier inaction by the Allies—after receipt of the Schulte/Riegner information—was based on wartime concerns, perhaps also latent anti-Semitism and other political reasons. Contributing to these facts, it should be added that the information received was so horrible that even people at the highest level of the U.S. government had difficulty

---

[66] See also www.holocaustchronicle.org. "1942: The Final Solution," page 295.

believing the news. Let me therefore not blame my poor father for not understanding the events as they unfolded!

If I had never heard the term "survivors' guilt," I would not have known of its existence. It may sound callous but I have never questioned why my parents and I were allowed to escape Germany at almost the last minute, and why so many others, including close relatives and friends, did not survive. I never considered myself a "superior" human being. I have just accepted the fact that it was my destiny to continue living and I never experienced any feelings of "guilt." In looking back, I can only say that I consider myself extremely lucky that I was the chosen one.

Throughout my writing, I have mentioned that my father's older sister and her husband were the people who supported my parents and me and were instrumental in rescuing us from Nazi Germany.

My aunt, a beautiful woman born to a poor Russian-Jewish family, had the great fortune that the wealthy son of a German-Jewish metal goods manufacturer fell in love with her. I do not know how this unlikely pair had met. Her eventual husband who took over the reins of the company after his father's death was not only an astute executive, but was also well-versed in German post-World War I politics. He also was madly in love with my aunt throughout his life. He later arranged with private tutors to "educate" this immigrant woman, to allow her to function in "upper" German society. She took lessons in the proper etiquette required of a woman of her new rank.

I previously mentioned that my uncle had realized early on the grave danger that Hitler represented. At a time when German Jews fully enjoyed the benefits of the Weimar Republic, he was the rare exception who perceived the coming changes and prepared for these eventualities.

His company, located in an industrial section of Berlin (Lichtenberg), produced small non-ferrous metal goods such as battery prongs, radio and telephone parts, the metal pieces for zippers, etc. A substantial portion of these items was exported to other, mostly European countries. The company employed in excess of 500 people.

The exports permitted my uncle over time to transfer at least a part of his liquid assets to a country that he had never visited, but one that he greatly admired, the USA. (The first time I was ever a passenger in a private car was in his American-built 1928 Packard Limousine.) By the time Hitler came to power, my uncle mentioned to me many years later, at least one million dollars of his were located in the U.S. In 2011 terms that would approximate more than 17 million dollars. Some of these funds were used to help his wife's family, and I am eternally grateful to him.

First reunion with my uncle and aunt, Ernst and Fanny
Kleinmann. We met in Los Angeles in December 1946
when I visited them on my leave from the U.S. Army. The
last time we had seen each other was in early 1934 in
Berlin.

14

SS *Navemar* and the Original Immigration Goal

IN THE SECTION "The Window Seat to Freedom," I described that in early 1940 my aunt had been able to obtain visas for our family allowing us to escape to the Dominican Republic, one of the few countries still accepting Jewish refugees.

I also mentioned that by spring 1941 my father and I had been informed that these visas had expired. As it happened, no German government official ever questioned the validity of the visas. Neither the Spanish nor Cuban consular people in Berlin examined the validity of the visas either; thus, we procured the all-important German exit permission as well as the transit visas for Spain and Cuba. Under the then-prevailing circumstances, I consider this a true miracle.

On July 21, 1941 we entered Spain, going first to Madrid, where we stayed for about three days, and then took a train to Seville. On August 5, we boarded the SS *Navemar* for the transatlantic crossing to Havana, Cuba.

A few days before that embarkation, another refugee boy (whom I had met in Seville) and I went to the harbor district, upon hearing that the SS *Navemar* had arrived. I had never seen an ocean-going vessel in my life except in pictures or in the movies. Therefore, I had no specific expectations regarding the *Navemar*. Yet, what I did see surprised me no end. Here was a 5,473t freighter built originally, I believe, either for intercoastal commerce or as a banana freighter. This tiny vessel was expected to carry between 1,100–1,200 passengers to Havana and New York.

The ship had originally been scheduled to sail from Cádiz. At the last moment, the embarkation place was changed to Seville. Much later I found out that the harbormaster in Cádiz had not permitted the departure from that port, correctly judging the ship not to be seaworthy. The harbormaster in Seville was more accommodating, perhaps with the help of dollars or pesetas lining his pockets. I have no knowledge of these shenanigans. It is still unbelievable to me that this tiny, overloaded freighter accomplished the seven-week voyage to Havana and New York.

When we finally boarded the ship, I realized what "improvements" the charterers had made to convert it into a passenger vessel. Originally, the *Navemar* had accommodations for about 20 or so people. That was all. The incoming refugee passengers were housed in the cargo holds of the vessel. That space had been changed into passenger accommodations by building wooden boxes. Approximately four holds allowed "sleeping quarters" for three hundred people each. We literally slept close to each other like sardines. It was also always warm in these holds since they were lacking in portholes. There were holds reserved for men and others for women and small children. For the entire trip, families were divided by sex.

Before continuing to explain the trip and our eventual arrival in Havana, I am inserting another epistle of the "exciting" times we endured.

Previously I had indicated that I have based considerable information contained in these writings upon my original 1941 letter to my friend Harry. He actually had considered an additional question but he did not feel it was appropriate to ask me—even after I had arrived in Havana. Harry and I met each other again around 1946 in New Jersey. Then he felt free to raise his final question: "Were you not afraid to sail for Cuba, after all that happened to the passengers on the *St. Louis*?"

The response to this surprising question was simple. Coming directly from Germany, my parents and I were only slightly familiar with that episode, but more importantly, we had no other choice. The trip to Cuba was literally our last possible salvation.

The "*St. Louis* affair" had started rather ordinarily. On May 13, 1939, the German MS *St. Louis* departed from Hamburg for Havana with about 900 Jewish refugees out of 937 passengers. Relatives and/or refugee organizations had purchased Cuban landing permits for these emigrants. The Cuban director of immigration apparently had sold these permits illegally. On May 5, prior to the departure of the *St. Louis* from Germany, the Cuban government under President Laredo Bru[67] had invalidated the permits without informing the permit holders or the German government. When the *St. Louis* arrived in Havana harbor on May 27, all but about 28 passengers were denied entry.

The German captain kept the ship in the harbor for about a week until forced out by Cuban authorities. All attempts by American refugee organizations to persuade the Cuban authorities to change their ruling proved useless.

Instead of turning around, the captain steered the

---

[67] Dr. Federico Laredo Bru was president of Cuba from 1936 to 1940. He was succeeded by Fulgencio Batista, the de facto leader of Cuba since 1933 and its elected president from 1940 to 1944. In 1944, Dr. Ramón Grau San Martín followed Batista as president. I lived in Cuba during the times that Batista and Grau were its presidents.

ship to Florida, hoping that perhaps the U.S. would accept the refugees. The Coast Guard, however, denied entrance into American waters. Direct appeals to the State Department and to President Roosevelt were ignored.

It was then that the captain of the *St. Louis* had no other alternative but to return to Europe. In literally the last minute and at the behest of some Jewish organizations, France, Great Britain, the Netherlands and Belgium agreed to accept all passengers. Except for those lucky ones who were taken to England, most of the remaining passengers were caught a year later in the onslaught of the European war and an estimated 254 of them ended up being killed by the Nazis.

The actions by the U.S. Coast Guard and the non-intervention by the State Department were not exactly shining moments of U.S. help to a tiny group of Jewish refugees. "The cruise of the *St. Louis* cries to high heaven of man's inhumanity to man," stated an editorial appearing at that time in *The New York Times*.

For those of us still in Germany it had become generally known that the *St. Louis* had been unable to discharge its passengers in Cuba. The valiant efforts of the German captain in trying to assist his Jewish passengers were obviously not publicized. We were, however, vaguely aware that the passengers were eventually permitted to disembark in western Europe and had not returned to Germany. These actions, including the guilt of the U.S., left a permanent mark on Jews *outside* of Germany, who knew much more about what had happened. This was the main reason Harry had delayed his question for so long.

It took 70 years, but the U.S. Senate passed a Resolution (S. Res. 111) stating in part:

> ...recognizing ... June 6, 2009, as the 70th anniversary of the tragic date when the MS *St.*

Louis, a ship carrying Jewish refugees from Nazi Germany, returned to Europe after its passengers were refused admittance to the United States and other countries in the Western Hemisphere. The Senate acknowledges the suffering of those refugees caused by the refusal of the United States, Cuban, and Canadian governments to provide them political asylum; and recognizing the 70th anniversary of the MS *St. Louis* tragedy as an opportunity for public officials and educators to raise awareness about an important historical event, the lessons of which are relevant to current and future generations.

The *Navemar* did not have enough refrigeration equipment for the food required for the seven-week journey for nearly 1,200 people. Therefore, the group who had chartered the ship took, if I remember correctly, about six live oxen on board. They were kept on deck, further reducing space for passengers, and at regular intervals one animal was killed (at night) to provide meat for all of us. The dead animal was hung on a yardarm, in full sight of everyone, before being butchered. I would not be surprised to hear that some passengers became vegetarians—but the handling of the meat did not bother me at all.

Considering the circumstances, the ship was relatively clean. The passengers themselves saw to that by organizing cleaning crews. Although there was no outbreak of any particular illness, the ship's only doctor was overwhelmed. Within a few days after the departure from Seville, however, a fair number of physicians among the refugees arranged to assist him. A number of people died on board. They were buried at sea during nighttime services. One pregnant woman was removed in Bermuda where her child was born.

In an article published by *The Royal Gazette and Colonist Daily* on August 30, 1941 when the *Navemar* docked in Hamilton, Bermuda before proceeding to Havana, a reporter stated,

> People who visited the ship yesterday tell of great discomfort but unconfined happiness. It is only possible to imagine the horrors of German concentration camps by watching the joy of people who, despite fierce hardships, revel in their freedom from the Nazi vice.

The *Navemar* also made headlines upon arriving in New York (after my parents and I and about 500 other refugees debarked in Cuba). Even *Time* magazine, in its weekly

N.Y. *Daily News*, Haberman-PM

S.S. NEVERMORE

Scenes like this reunion were the bright side of the picture when the grimy Spanish freighter *Navemar* came to port in New York Harbor last week. Seven long weeks before, she had cleared from Seville, with a miserable human cargo, mostly war refugees. Built to accommodate 28 passengers, she had packed 1,120 aboard, into her hold and every usable part of the ship. Some of them had paid scalpers as much as $1,750 for their unforgettable passage.

According to their stories, they sickened on rotten food. In crude bunks they lay for days, some of them stricken with fever. Six died. Many slept in lifeboats (*left*) rather than endure the stinking hold. One physician said it was a "miracle" no epidemic broke out. They nicknamed their ship the *Nevermore*.

issue of September 22, 1941, carried a short article about the ship, shown on the previous page; the text also appears on page 191. Some details of the account differ from my own recollections, but nevertheless the overall picture is as I remember it.

The tickets for the three of us cost about $1,200 each. In today's dollars that would equal in excess of $60,000 in total. This turned out to be one of the worst scandals in the shipping industry at that time. The few other ships still transferring refugees to the Western Hemisphere also charged exorbitant prices but the *Navemar* topped all of them in price and in deplorable conditions. Upon arriving in New York, some American lawyers preferred charges against the lessees of the ship. Several years later, my parents received a total refund of about two or three hundred dollars.

While crossing the Atlantic the *Navemar* was brightly illuminated at night, flying the neutral Spanish flag. However, on her return trip from New York to Spain a submarine (probably German or Italian) torpedoed her although she was still marked as a neutral ship. She was not carrying any passengers at that time.

The *Navemar* discharged the Cuban-bound refugees, about 500, at Havana harbor on September 6, 1941. The entire group was taken to the Immigration Camp in Tiscornia on the outskirts of Havana (Cuba's Ellis Island). The camp, while guarded, was a "paradise" in comparison to the *Navemar*. It was clean, quite well administered and the food served was plain but sufficient. In record time, I think less than a week, the entire group was discharged after all documents and luggage had been inspected. I believe my parents and I were released after about three or four days. I still vividly remember that the paper discharging us from the camp had a statement attached that we could only be released "if we were in possession of a valid visa for the Dominican Republic." Here again the Cuban authorities followed the European ones and no one realized that the Dominican visas had expired.

From the camp, we were taken in an immigration bus to a taxi station in the center of Havana. There we were told that we were free to leave. From the evening of July 18, 1941 when we left Berlin until that moment in early September, we had always been under someone's control. Earlier I had mentioned the wagon "for Jews only." In Paris, a German-speaking French employee of an international refugee organization was put in charge of the people in the wagon. He accompanied the group via Madrid to Seville. There another member of a refugee organization assigned us to a hotel.

On a daily basis, we were kept abreast regarding the eventual transatlantic crossing. Finally, on the date of departure, we were taken to the harbor where we boarded the SS *Navemar*. In Havana, as I had mentioned, we were escorted *en masse* to the immigration camp. Now, suddenly and without any warning, one and a half months after our departure from Nazi Germany, my parents and I were on our own. There was no aid worker from a refugee organization at the taxi stop. We found ourselves stranded in a strange city, without any knowledge of the language (except for my school Spanish), carrying a few suitcases and worst of all without any money except for some dollars that my aunt had wired us to Tiscornia. We were frightened and bewildered. We did not know where to go or what to do.

At the immigration camp, we had overheard that a reasonably-priced hotel in the center of the city was called Hotel Inglaterra. Therefore, we took a taxi to that hotel. Arriving at the Inglaterra, we were advised that it was fully booked. The taxi driver then suggested the Hotel

Montserrat located within a few blocks and in a similar price range. This turned out to be an extremely lucky break; I wish I could thank the unknown Cuban taxi driver for his recommendation.

Literally within days of our arrival, the mother of the hotel owner "fell in love" with us and we stayed at that place until we immigrated to the USA three years and seven months later. Because we were refugees and without any visible means of support, Sra. Rodríguez viuda de Garcia arranged with her son to charge us an extremely modest rent, including three meals daily. I believe we paid around 90 dollars monthly (about $1,500 in today's dollars). We could not have lived less expensively anywhere in Cuba.

Mrs. Rodríguez was a simple woman with a big heart. She had immigrated to Cuba many years earlier with her husband and eventually became the owner of a modest hotel, now managed by her son. She was shocked by the events that had befallen her native Spain, particularly the Spanish Civil War, and the advent of General Franco had left a deep mark on her. She had a profound understanding and feeling of what it meant to have had to leave one's native land. My parents did not speak Spanish and Mrs. Rodríguez spoke no language other than Spanish. Yet, somehow, a close friendship developed between the three of them. (My mother eventually was able to speak some Spanish while my father never did.) Many years later, Mrs. Rodríguez visited my parents in New Jersey.

Our goal, or better said our expectation, after having arrived in Havana was still to settle in the Dominican Republic. Within about two weeks, we had obtained new, valid Dominican visas. It was late September 1941; the original Cuban permission to stay was for 30 days, then renewed for periods of 30 days. Now my aunt and uncle advised us to remain in Cuba "for a short time longer" and that arrangements would be made to allow us to immigrate to the USA. This plan came to a sudden end on December 7 with the Japanese attack on the U.S., which was followed by Germany declaring war against the U.S. Since Cuba, then a close ally of the U.S., had also declared war on Japan and Germany, as Germans we had overnight become "enemy aliens" in both Cuba and the U.S.

Immigration to the U.S. for enemy aliens was temporarily stopped. However, Cuba's Fulgencio Batista signed a law allowing all refugees to stay in Cuba for the duration of the war. Immigration to the U.S. was resumed around 1943/44, and by the beginning of 1945 we were finally in possession of the visas allowing us to permanently settle in the U.S.

We certainly had not missed anything by staying in Cuba instead of continuing to the Dominican Republic. A little research bears this out. The original visa for the Dominican Republic, shown on page 27, states that we can enter the Dominican Republic "... in accordance with the contract for the establishment of homesteaders" (*Según contrato para el establecimiento de colonos*). What did that mean?

An advertising brochure published on the Internet[68] discusses a popular beach area in the Dominican Republic, "Sosúa." I am citing one short paragraph:

> Opposite of the bay is El Batey which is booming with new hotels and tourist attractions. It was founded in 1940 when the dictator Trujillo, seeking goodwill from the international community after having ordered the massacre of almost 20,000 Haitians in the country, offered to take in Jewish

---

[68] Originally obtained at www.hispaniola.com. This text no longer appears there but is found on other travel websites.

refugees from Germany who were being persecuted by the Nazis. About 600 of them immigrated, of whom only a small group eventually remained and became engaged in the dairy and smoked-meat industries.

To understand this citation fully we have to go back a little further into history. In July 1938, at the initiative of President Franklin Roosevelt, representatives of about 31 countries gathered at the French spa in Evian-les-Bains to discuss the problem of "refugees." (They were not referred to as "Jews" at that time!) At the conference one could hear lots of expressions of sympathy from all the representatives but no actual help from any of the countries, including the U.S. The latter simply pledged that it would allow the full quota of German and Austrian immigrants of about 27,370 per year to enter the country. Except for the year 1939, even this relatively small quota was not fully used because of American red tape.[69]

It is now believed that this inaction by the world community effectively sealed the fate of the European Jews. After the conclusion of the conference, Hitler is said to have declared that "...in Evian, the myth of the international Jewish strength and influence was shattered." The non-intervention by the rest of the world was a *sine qua non* for the success of the "Final Solution of the Jewish Problem."[70] My own aunt's earlier-cited prediction that nobody would be interested in the fate of the German Jews unfortunately had turned into reality.

---

[69] Bat-Ami Zucker, *In Search of Refuge. Jews and U.S. Consuls in Nazi Germany 1933-1941*. Portland, Oregon: Valentine Mitchell, 2001. Quoted in *Together*, January 2003. Published by the "American Gathering of Jewish Holocaust Survivors," New York, NY, Volume 16 Number 3, page 12.

[70] See also Policy Dispatch No. 30 "Sixty years after Evian," published by the World Jewish Congress, July 1998.

Yet, there was one notable exception to this inaction. The representative of the Dominican Republic, Sr. Virgilio Molina, declared that for colonization purposes his country had at its disposal large areas of fertile land and would be prepared to make its contribution by granting special advantageous concessions to Austrian and German exiles.

In further negotiations with that country and the American Joint Agricultural Corporation (a subsidiary of the United Jewish Appeal), which volunteered to finance the settlement project, a Dominican Republic Settlement Association (DORSA) was formed. Dr. Joseph A. Rosen of DORSA went to that country and selected a 26,000-acre tract at Sosúa. That town is located in the heart of a beach area on the North Coast of the Dominican Republic, about 20 km (32 miles) east of Puerto Plata. That was the contract for the establishment of homesteaders, referred to in our visas. Nowadays a street in the center of Sosúa carries the name "Dr. Rosen." There is also a small synagogue in Sosúa, possibly the only one to appear in the central part of a town in Latin America, where usually a Catholic church is the main attraction of the inner city.

The first settlers arrived in May 1940 and founded a flourishing settlement. However, the war in Europe had started. Therefore, only about 660 immigrants ever reached the country out of the 100,000 that would have been allowed to enter. Among the papers of one of the settlers whose family donated his accounts to the Leo Baeck Institute in New York I have found the following summary:

> It costs DORSA around $2,000 to establish a family on a homestead, which includes a house on three acres of land, three additional acres of garden land, furniture, and garden tools; small livestock, a horse,

a mule, a saddle, two cows, miscellaneous equipment, plus credit for a project approved by DORSA.

About 5–6,000 visas are estimated to have been issued in total. I assume, therefore, that in addition to the 660 immigrants that actually arrived in the Dominican Republic several hundred additional people (like my parents and me) were saved from the Nazis by using these visas. This offer had come from a dictator who was called a bastard or worse by many—and supposedly "our" bastard by President Roosevelt.

I visited Sosúa-El Batey in April 2004 and, having seen the place, I became more convinced than ever that my parents and I would not have been happy living and working in that area. Yet, I am forever grateful to Trujillo and his cohorts. They, in effect, saved my life. The original visa to the Dominican Republic set the emigration from Germany in motion. At the time we left Nazi Germany, this was the last and only way open for us.

I should mention one final episode regarding my "relationship" with the Dominican Republic. In 1957, shortly after I had been appointed an assistant comptroller of the International Division of Olin-Mathieson Chemical Corporation, I was sent on an urgent assignment to that country. I stayed at one of the best hotels and was "royally" treated by the branch manager of our company, as well as by some of Olin's major customers in Ciudad Trujillo (now Santo Domingo). A visitor from the New York home office was still a rarity at that time.

Early one morning I was not permitted to leave the hotel in order to go to the Olin office. Sr. Trujillo had decided to take a stroll in the area where the hotel was located, and therefore the street was closed for about half an hour. But I did get a glimpse at the Generalissimo.

I have no specific recollection of the assignment that had required my presence in the Dominican Republic. There were, I somehow recall, problems regarding inventory controls (Olin sold fertilizer to the Dominican farmers) and the collectability of outstanding accounts receivable. I do remember, however, that whatever recommendations I did suggest were accepted. The branch manager even wrote a letter of appreciation to the New York headquarters about my visit. The success of that trip to the Dominican Republic helped me greatly in my career advancement. For the second time in my life, this small, desperately poor country in the Caribbean played a major role in my personal well-being.

Postcard of the Montserrat Hotel

In Front of the Olin-Mathieson Office
(my first trip to the Dominican Republic, around 1957)

15

The End of the Emigration Odyssey

THE PAN-AMERICAN Airways plane NC 33320 landed in Miami, Florida on April 23, 1945. The trip from Havana, my first airplane ride, probably lasted no more than 90 minutes. Yet, it covered a whole world; 1,375 days had passed since we had left Berlin!

Clearing customs and immigration formalities took hours; at least it seemed that way. We were, after all, "enemy aliens" arriving in the USA and seeking permanent residence status while the war against Germany was still being fought. The customs officer examined our three suitcases, the same ones we had taken out of Germany, in greatest detail. The immigration official was not particularly friendly either. He must have thought he was

The receipt for my father's immigration tax

NOT REFUNDABLE   **NO REEMBOLSABLE**

Received of HERMANN BURSTEIN $8.00 U. S. Currency
RECIBIDO DE   Moneda de EE. UU. de A.

IN PAYMENT OF U. S. IMMIGRATION HEAD TAX
En pago de Impuesto de Entrada del Depto. de Inmigración de los EE. UU. de A.

PASSENGER ARRIVED FROM HAV ON NC 33320 ON 4/23 1945
Que Llegó de _____ en el Avión,
         W. A. Johnson
         Traffic Representative

FORM E81-808 (V-88) PASSENGER COPY

talking to the enemy. My parents' knowledge of the English language was poor to say the least. Therefore, I had become the interpreter. The immigration officer gave me two major instructions. He admonished me to be absolutely sure to register for the draft within 72 hours after our arrival in New Jersey, our ultimate destination. He also instructed my parents and me to report to the nearest FBI office (in Newark, NJ) and to register as enemy aliens. I believe the time span for reporting to the FBI was set at seven days. That later visit to the FBI was a terrible ordeal for my parents because they had to enter a federal police office, which they somehow associated with the Gestapo. It actually turned out to be a short, business-like affair. We were photographed and fingerprinted and also each received a small booklet attesting to the fact that we had registered. The FBI employee advised us to carry it with us at all times. I had to surrender my own booklet upon being drafted into the U.S. Army eight months later, when I ceased to be an "enemy alien."

Finally, we were admitted to this country under Section 6A3 of the Immigration Act of 1924. At the airport we were met by two extremely pleasant and helpful women, volunteers from a Jewish welfare organization. These ladies escorted us to the Hotel Miami. Their welcome assistance took the sting out of the rather cold reception we had received so far. I wish I could thank them again. They represented everything that is good in this country. The next morning they gave us a sightseeing tour of the city. The following day one of them picked me up for a swim at her club. Lastly, they accompanied us to the railroad station and we took the "Silver Meteor" to New York. No Jewish wagon this time and no drawn curtains. We were free to use the dining car, as long as we were able to pay, and we had two window seats without having asked for them!

After a trip of about 26 hours, we were welcomed at Pennsylvania Station in New York by my mother's oldest sister, Sara Golz, who had immigrated with her two sons to the U.S. in the late 1920s. She had followed her husband who had left Germany about six years earlier. Also greeting us was a small group of other, mostly "unknown" relatives. Lunch at a dairy restaurant in midtown Manhattan was followed by a trip to my aunt's house in North Bergen, NJ. My cousin Sam was driving. As we emerged from the Lincoln Tunnel he pointed to the New York side. To this day I consider that view of Manhattan one of the most beautiful sights in the world.

We were in heaven although afraid of the future. As hard as it might have been living in Cuba, from one check to another donated by extremely dear and helpful relatives, it was actually a carefree experience. I did office work—typing and translating—and worked part-time for a German-language immigrant weekly newspaper *Unterwegs* (On the Way), while attending a Cuban high school for Arts and Crafts (*Escuela Superior de Artes y Oficios*). My starting salary was ten cents an hour, later increased to $1.00 per day for about four to six hours of work. Both my parents found occasional part-time employment. Papa did electrical repairs and Mutti worked as a seamstress. (Foreigners could not legally work in Cuba without specific authorization by the Ministry of Labor that was difficult to obtain, and all work my parents or I did was strictly "off the books.")

After breakfast, on the first morning after our arrival in New Jersey, "Tante Sali" (as I called my aunt) asked me for a favor. She gave me some small change (a loaf of bread at that time cost nine cents) and requested that I go to the corner grocery store, literally only a few houses away, and buy a "Jewish rye." I questioned her, repeating the words "a Jewish rye," emphasizing the word

136

"Jewish." Tante Sali did not quite understand my concern and simply responded: "Yes, a Jewish rye, because it tastes better."

So I went on my first shopping mission in this country. I was extremely disturbed to ask a store clerk for a *Jewish* rye. The war in Europe was in its last two weeks. There was no doubt in my mind it meant the end of the Nazi regime in Germany as well as the end of the European part of the war. We had also finally arrived at our ultimate destination and were living in a free country. In spite of all these positive events the simple act of having to utter the word "Jewish" to a stranger evoked terrible memories in me. I was practically shaking when I got to the grocery store and, in a trembling voice, asked for that Jewish rye.

It was an unusual reaction to a rather simple request. However, the fear of associating myself in public as a Jew was obviously still with me. The clerk nonchalantly pointed to the particular bread rack. I grabbed the bread, paid him and left the store in a hurry. I have never forgotten that experience.

Within a few days after our arrival, my father and I started to look for work. That search turned out to be the easiest part—contrary to the experiences of many immigrants at that time. My father obtained his first job as a night watchman at a fur dyeing company owned by one of the distant relatives that had met us at the railroad station. Prior to my arrival, and unknown to me, my cousin Sam had arranged with one of his former employers to hire me as a mechanic's helper. That job lasted only about six weeks. Mr. Pine was not happy with my mechanical aptitude—he was right—and I was not happy because my work included washing and waxing his car. However, the war in the Pacific was still in progress, so I had no difficulty in obtaining other relatively low-paying jobs in machine shops throughout the summer and fall of 1945—until I was drafted into the U.S. Army. (I also attended high school classes at night.) We moved to a modest apartment in Guttenberg, NJ where I lived, except for my Army service, until I got married. My mother also found work as a tailor. She had not worked in Germany since I was born. Yet, she eventually became the forelady in a women's garment factory, a job she held until her premature death at the age of 63.

The words "civil rights" were not a part of my vocabulary at that time. The concept of "equal opportunity" was also unknown to me. However, I had a nagging feeling that these United States had severe problems, which I could not then adequately define but which greatly disturbed me.

I had escaped from a Germany that had erected signs stating "Jews Not Welcome" or worse. On the first full day after my arrival in the USA when the two nice ladies took my parents and me on a sightseeing trip, I saw—at the courthouse in Miami of all places—under a huge picture of the goddess of justice (with her eyes covered as if she were ashamed)—two identical water fountains. To my great surprise and disappointment I noticed a sign attached to one of these fountains. It read "For Coloreds Only." The problems that later besieged this country with regard to its minority population did not come as a shock to me. I felt them coming at that moment and it saddened me immensely.

16

Meeting Otto

ONE EVENT, WHICH I shall not forget, happened many years after the end of the Holocaust but is closely related to that horrible era.

On March 20, 1995 Japanese terrorists, the Aum Shinrikyo cult, released the nerve gas sarin into the Tokyo subway system. Some newspapers incorrectly explained that sarin and a related gas, tabun, had been developed by the Nazis for use in the gas chambers. In a letter to the editor of *The New York Times*, published on March 28, 1995, a Mr. R. H. Hodges—whom the paper identified as a long-time researcher into the Nazi regime—described the two gases and clarified their Nazi connection. Mr. Hodges explained that the two gases had been discovered as early as 1902. They were patented in 1937/38 by I. G. Farbenindustrie (I. G. Farben),[71] the German industrial giant, and they were later refined by the Nazis. While the gases were never used in the war effort, in May 1943, several prominent Nazi leaders (Dr. Goebbels among them) urged their use on the Russian front after the debacle of Stalingrad, and by the fall of 1944, the same Nazis tried to convince Hitler to use tabun on western

---

[71] The full name of the company was *Interessen Gemeinschaft Farbenindustrie Aktiengesellschaft* (Community of Interest of Dye Manufacturing Companies).

enemy cities and other installations.[72]

According to Hodges, Hitler relied in both instances upon the advice of a certain Dr. Otto Ambros, member of I. G. Farben's board and an expert on poison gas. Ambros advised Hitler not to use any poison gas on either the eastern or western fronts, and reminded him that the Allies had a greater capacity to produce these gases. In fact, Hodges claimed that Ambros's estimate of the Allies' chemical warfare capability was wrong, and that the introduction of either gas might have altered the course of the war.

While Hitler rejected the use of sarin and tabun against the Allies, it remained "permissible" to continue to use poison gas—Zyklon B—on Jews! A company related to I. G. Farben produced that gas.[73]

---

[72] Tabun and sarin were developed by I. G. Farben for military use. Dr. Otto Ambros, a rising star in the company, had assumed responsibility for the production of these two gases for the German armed forces. See also Diarmuid Jeffreys, *Hell's Cartel*, Henry Holt and Company, New York, 2008.

[73] The German-Jewish physical chemist Fritz Haber received the Nobel Prize in Chemistry in 1918 for his direct synthesis of ammonia from nitrogen and hydrogen. This World War I achievement had freed Germany from its dependence on nitrate imports from Chile in order to produce nitrogen fertilizers and munitions. During the same war, Haber defended and assisted German poison gas warfare—a decision that led his wife Clara to commit suicide. Clara was a physical chemist who received her PhD in 1900, probably the first one in that field awarded to a woman. She had regarded her husband's involvement in chemical warfare as an abomination of science and a sign of barbarism. Haber became the chief of the German chemical warfare service in 1916. During the 1920s, he developed the Zyklon B cyanamide gas as an insecticide. It would be put to work, some 15 years later, in the Nazi extermination centers. Haber died in 1934 in Switzerland after being forced out of Nazi Germany a year earlier, and did not live to see the horrific outcome of his labors. Several members of his own family were killed by Zyklon B gas. Strangely enough though, on January 29, 1935, one year after his death, the Kaiser Wilhelm Institute for Chemistry in Berlin, with the help of I. G. Farben chief executive Carl Bosch and in defiance of an explicit government prohibition, held a memorial service for Haber. The 1918 Nobel laureate for physics Max Planck and the

Hodges's letter to the editor was not the first time I had heard of Dr. Otto Ambros, though it was the first time I learned of his interactions with Hitler. After reading the letter, I contacted Mr. Hodges and corresponded with him regarding a strange meeting I once had with that same Dr. Otto Ambros.

In the fall of 1971 I was elected a vice president of W. R. Grace & Co. About a month later, I was asked to accompany a Grace contingent (headed by the late J. Peter Grace) to a European conference in Lausanne, Switzerland. The first day began with a luncheon for all participants. While we were waiting to be seated, the then-chief financial officer of the corporation, my immediate superior, introduced me to some of the attendees; thus, I met Dr. Otto Ambros.

Ambros was serving as a consultant for Grace. I had never heard his name before. I was also completely unaware of his background. My boss told us emphatically that we should sit next to each other since we were both "Germans." The officer most certainly knew of Ambros's background; yet, I am convinced he did not realize at that moment what he was suggesting.

Speaking in German, Otto Ambros and I spent an amazing time, more than two hours, together. We talked about a wide range of topics: the economy, music, the Grace operations, etc. I admired his intelligence, his charm

---

physical chemist Otto Hahn (a 1944 Nobel Prize winner for discovering nuclear fission) were among the approximately 500 distinguished participants. I believe this was probably the only time a Jew was honored in Nazi Germany. In his introductory remarks, Professor Planck pointed out that had Haber not made his ammonia synthesis discovery, Germany would have collapsed, economically and militarily, in the first three months of World War I. Albert Einstein was quoted in *Master Mind* (Harper Collins New York, 2005), page 239: "At the end, he was forced to experience all the bitterness of being abandoned by the people of his circle ... It was the tragedy of the German Jew: the tragedy of unrequited love."

and his wit. And I had the distinct feeling that our admiration was mutual.

One topic we did not touch—as if by unspoken agreement—was the Nazi era in Germany. Since Ambros was older than I, it seemed only natural to me that he had participated in some way in the war effort and that he might possibly have been a member of the Nazi party.[74] I had mentioned to him the date I had left Germany, so he obviously knew that I was Jewish; in 1941, no non-Jew of military age would have been permitted to leave Germany.

Towards the end of the luncheon Ambros put his arm around me and exclaimed how wonderful it was that we could enjoy each other's company "after all that had happened in Germany." My rather simple answer was that I could never forget what had happened but I would not hold every single German responsible for the past. Ambros nodded his agreement.[75]

At that time I did not yet know that I had spent a remarkable and enjoyable time with a man who had probably not participated in any killings personally, but

---

[74] Around the time the Nazis assumed power in Germany, they did not accept any additional membership in the party. This prohibition was lifted in 1937, after which time a person's decision to join the party might have been based on political or economic or other "practical" concerns. At that time, Otto Ambros became a member. Those who had joined before 1933 had presumably become Nazis from conviction. At least until 1941 (when I left Germany), members from before 1933 were considered *alte Kämpfer* (old fighters) and considered themselves the "better" Nazis.

[75] Years later, in a passionate speech addressing President Reagan in order to dissuade him from visiting the Bitburg military cemetery in Germany where SS officers were buried, the Holocaust survivor and Peace Nobelist Elie Wiesel expressed his feelings about the Germans in simple language, but more succinctly than I had formulated it. He said: "I do not believe in collective guilt, nor in collective responsibility. Only the killers were guilty." For a complete text of the speech and a short explanation of the historical connection surrounding it, see *In Our Own Words: Extraordinary Speeches of the American Century*, edited by Senator Robert Torricelli and Andrew Carroll (New York: Kodansha International America, Inc., 1999, pp. 363–366).

who had been most instrumental in facilitating the killing machine.[76]

Afterwards, we parted company. I never saw Otto Ambros again.

A short while later, back in New York, while talking to another Grace officer who had not attended the European conference, I mentioned my meeting with Ambros. That man informed me that one reason for staging the Grace management meeting in Switzerland was the fact that even at that time, 26 years after the end of World War II, Otto Ambros—a convicted major Nazi war criminal—was not permitted entrance into the USA. However, J. Peter Grace supposedly had wanted Ambros to participate in the meeting because of his vast knowledge and connections (!) within the German chemical industry.

Having heard this, I made an effort to obtain further information about my erstwhile luncheon partner. I learned that on April 7, 1941 (incidentally my last birthday while in Nazi Germany) Dr. Otto Ambros spoke at the groundbreaking ceremony for a new factory being constructed in the village of Monowitz, adjacent to Auschwitz, Poland. A concentration camp had been operating in Auschwitz since May 1940. Ambros declared at the groundbreaking that

> ...the plan developed by I. G. Farbenindustrie for "Project Auschwitz" foresees a giant enterprise ... using our best resources we are determined to establish a living company and we will use all our power that this Auschwitz organization becomes a solid cornerstone for a powerful and healthy Germanic presence in the East.[77]

---

[76] Between 1942 and 1944, Ambros visited Auschwitz on 18 separate occasions, sometimes staying several days. It is inconceivable that he did not know what was happening, as he stated after the end of the war.
[77] See also *Die Zeit*, dated March 3, 1991, for a fascinating article by Otto

Ambros was referring to two factories that were being erected for the production of Buna (a synthetic rubber) and for gasoline derived from coal.[78] At that time, he was a member of the board of I. G. Farben and was the official responsible for this project. He had selected Monowitz as the location of these new operations, "reasoning" that he could obtain any number of "cheap" laborers from the Auschwitz concentration camp that was conveniently located nearby. By the fall of 1942, the factory site had expanded to include its own barracks, and it then became a labor camp—known variously as I. G. Auschwitz, Auschwitz-Monowitz, Auschwitz-Buna, or Auschwitz III—and was a prominent part of the sprawling Auschwitz complex that ultimately included three main camps and forty-five "sub-camps."[79]

A U.S. military court in Germany sentenced Otto Ambros on May 12, 1948 to a prison term of eight years for slavery and mass murder. During the trial Ambros never admitted to any participation in the crimes at Auschwitz. He became one of about twelve former I. G. Farbenindustrie officials convicted. Pardoned in 1950 because of "good behavior," he served less than half his sentence.[80] At the trial, it had been established that neither

---

Köhler under the title *Hochstimmung im Schatten der I. G. Auschwitz* (High Spirits in the Shadow of I. G. Auschwitz).

[78] At the Paris International Exposition in 1937, "Buna" had received a gold medal, and Ambros was in his glory.

[79] The most well-known was Auschwitz II, or Auschwitz-Birkenau, the notorious death camp at which approximately one million people were murdered, ninety percent of them Jews.

[80] It is more than unfortunate that the man who had the responsibility for the location, planning and running of "I. G. Auschwitz" and also had materially created Nazi Germany's secret chemical weapons program went on—after his release from prison—as chairman or member of the boards of a large number of companies such as Berliner Handelsgesellschaft, Chemie Grünenthal, Knoll A. G., Pintsch Bamag, Süddeutsche Kalkstickstoffwerke and many others. He also became an adviser on chemical matters to the German government in Bonn and,

the SS nor any other German governmental organization had forced upon him his choice of Auschwitz-Monowitz for the location of the factories. Higher profit for his company was his only motive.[81] Ernst Michel, an Auschwitz survivor who had worked for two years at Auschwitz-Buna, stated that about 30,000 concentration camp inmates died at that complex while working for I. G. Farben.[82]

At the beginning of this chapter, I mentioned that I had never heard of Otto Ambros before my "enjoyable" meeting with him. The question might then be raised: would I have handled myself differently had I been aware of his background?

I truly do not know the answer to this legitimate concern. I have to consider that I had just recently joined W. R. Grace & Co. as a corporate vice president. I was married at that time and had to support a wife and three teenage girls. In other words, I could ill afford to insult a

---

last but not least, a consultant to W. R. Grace & Co.

[81] In October 1943, the first tanker load of methanol was driven out through the gates of I. G. Farben's Auschwitz factories. The remaining work proceeded extremely slowly, hampered by raw material shortages, mechanical breakdowns and of course the weakened workforce. From about the middle of 1944 there were also air raids by the U.S. Air Force. Overall, Ambros's "Project Auschwitz" turned out to be a complete failure. It resulted in a death toll of at least 30,000 inmates as estimated by survivor Ernst Michel (other estimates talk of anywhere from 40,000 to 200,000 people). About 900 million Reichsmark are said to have been spent on the construction of the factories. By the time the Soviet forces captured Auschwitz on January 27, 1945, with the exception of some methanol not a single pound of Buna rubber or one liter of synthetic gasoline were ever produced.

[82] Well-known prisoners at Auschwitz-Buna included Nobel laureate Elie Wiesel and Italian writer Primo Levi. Additional information regarding Otto Ambros and his Auschwitz–I. G. Farben dream is available in Newsletter 15, fall 1998, issued by Fritz Bauer Institut, Frankfurt/M, Germany (the Newsletter is published in the German language). Other details are available in *Lifestyles*, international edition, winter 1999, vol. 28, no. 164, Lifestyles Magazine USA, Inc. Buffalo, NY. The most detailed study is presented in *Hell's Cartel*, previously mentioned.

man who had legally "paid" for his crimes, no matter how much I might have despised him. At least, I probably would have tried to ignore him altogether. That might have been a cowardly way of treating him. Yet, under the circumstances, I doubt I would have gone any further.

17

My Service in the U.S. Army

DRAFTED INTO THE Army on December 10, 1945 I reported that morning at the draft board in North Bergen, New Jersey. I was bussed, with some 30 other young men, to the old Induction Center on Whitehall Street in lower Manhattan. That center operated from 1884 to 1969. There we were in the words of Arlo Guthrie's song *Alice's Restaurant* "injected, inspected, detected, infected, neglected and selected."

Together with a group of about 80 men, I was taken by bus to a reception camp in New Jersey and several days later to Ft. Bragg, North Carolina for basic training, which took place from December 1945 to February 16, 1946. At the conclusion of the training, all of the people in my group were transferred to an Air Force base for deployment overseas. All, except for me! Under the then-existing laws, non-citizens drafted into the Armed Forces were entitled to become U.S. citizens upon successful completion of their basic military training. There were about eight or ten soldiers with me who took the oath of citizenship on March 5, 1946 in a brief ceremony at the Cumberland County Court House in Fayetteville, NC. The presiding judge interrupted a murder trial to swear us in, telling us that we were already good citizens because we were defending the country. At this point, I became a citizen in a little more than ten months after having arrived in the USA.

For the several weeks between the end of basic training and the swearing-in ceremony and shortly thereafter, I was, in Army parlance, "unassigned," staying in a semi-empty barrack. However, the Army saw to it that I should be "productive." Therefore, I became the glazier for several blocks within the Ft. Bragg compound. Every morning around 9 AM, I received a pail, some tools, putty and panels of window glass. I would then walk from barrack to barrack looking for broken windowpanes, which I had to replace. This was not necessarily the best use of my talents. It took me probably several hours to replace the first windowpane, though I became somewhat more efficient as time passed. Yet, I got plenty of fresh air, and could work at my own pace without any supervision. In the evenings, I was free to go to the movies or to the library. Shortly thereafter, the work detail ended and I was transferred to Camp Kilmer, NJ to await further orders. That latter waiting period lasted from March until October.

Practically every weekend I was permitted to go home, visiting my parents and my friends. During the workweek, because of my typing skills, I was assigned as an assistant company clerk, typing reports and doing other office work, which was much more to my liking than replacing windowpanes. Nevertheless, I saw no future in wasting my time at that place. However, I was in a headquarters office and had become acquainted with the other cadre. I also had developed a good working relationship with the captain of the unit. My "coworkers" mentioned to me that the Counter Intelligence Corps (CIC) was looking for agents with knowledge of foreign languages. By that time, I also had acquired some familiarity with Army regulations, and a lot of chutzpah. I wrote a letter to the Commanding Officer of the CIC, "through channels" and approved by Captain Gworek, my unit chief, requesting a transfer to that organization.

I never received any acknowledgement of my letter. However, in October I was transferred to the CIC in Baltimore. From mid-November until graduation on March 14, 1947 I underwent a rather strenuous but enjoyable course of instruction, literally kept busy from early morning until late at night. I did not know it at that time but when I entered college, I would receive six credits towards my degree for the time spent at the CIC school. I learned how to operate a variety of hand weapons, rifles and machine guns, open locks (called "surreptitious methods of entry"), how to check for concealed weapons and interrogate prisoners, how to disarm a person with a weapon pointed at me and other "interesting" subjects. Most of these skills were never needed in my Army career. Two hours daily were consumed by basic Russian; that helped many years later when I visited the former Soviet Union and was at least able to read the street signs. There were one or two other privates attending the school with me but the majority of my fellow students consisted of higher-ranking enlisted men with many years of Army service. It was an intelligent and congenial group, very different from the men I had encountered at basic training.

Soon after graduation, I was on my way to occupied Germany—back to the country which I had left under such traumatic circumstances less than six years earlier. Leaving Bremerhaven where the ship anchored I found myself on a U.S. troop train on the way to Marburg, and about a week or two later to Oberursel (near Frankfurt/M)—then the European Intelligence Headquarters for the U.S. Army— where I was finally stationed for about a year.

At first, it was a strange feeling to be on German soil again, to hear people on the street speaking German and to see street signs in German. I did not feel any hatred towards the people but I also realized that I could never belong to that country again.

On my first free day, still in Marburg, I went to visit a castle and, purely by chance, the only other people at the place were a few GIs who had difficulty communicating with the elderly docent who only spoke German. I came to the rescue and actually enjoyed my first excursion. Then I was off to Oberursel together with my fellow graduates from Baltimore. Within a few days, the group was split up and assigned to various CIC posts within the U.S. Zone of Occupation. Everyone received specific orders, even those few who stayed at headquarters. Everyone—but me!

Called in by the sergeant major I was told in a rather nasty way that I was going to be transferred out of the CIC because I had not been a U.S. citizen for at least ten years as required by that organization. This was a blunt lie; every CIC agent of German-Jewish background whom I had met at either Baltimore or Oberursel had been a citizen for much less than ten years. I was never able to find the cause of the sergeant major's behavior. I guess that "someone" may have expressed doubts about my reliability because I had only lived in the U.S. for a few months, although that fact had certainly been known before I even received my orders to report to Baltimore for training.

I was devastated. To add insult to injury, the sergeant major stated that the U.S. Army headquarters in Frankfurt needed German-speaking guards, and he ordered me to report to the guard section for an interview. Luckily, the sergeant at headquarters did not like me and I was not accepted (this was the only rejection I ever liked).

That evening I ate at the mess hall with a friend from Baltimore who was temporarily assigned to the CIC in Oberursel. I discussed my unhappiness with him. That fellow, a French Canadian from Massachusetts (I only remember his last name, de la Riviere) had studied for several semesters at Tufts University before being drafted into the Army. He was not only very sympathetic, but he was able to help me. He mentioned that he had met that very day a former professor of his who had become a civilian employee of the Army, also stationed in Oberursel. The professor, now in charge of a Military Intelligence Section, had told my friend that he was looking for a good German-speaking person. The next day, meeting Mr. Singer—to whom my friend introduced me—saved my sanity. After my long and frank talk with him, Mr. Singer stated that he would try to arrange for my transfer to his group. Within a day or two he succeeded, and I became the youngest member (and the only soldier) of a fascinating, secret unit.

I was assigned a small private office and had a WAC sergeant secretary. At that time, my own rank was Private First Class. (My friend called me the highest-ranking private in the U.S. Army.) My new job consisted of translating certain secret German papers into English. Literally overnight from possibly being judged unfit for a CIC position, I had a secret clearance and an important new assignment.

The former head of the German World War II *Abteilung Fremde Heere Ost* (Section Foreign Armies East) at the Russian front had surrendered, together with his unit and all its documents, to the U.S. forces in the spring of 1945. This man, Major General Reinhard Gehlen, was an opportunist and agreed to work for U.S. Military Intelligence and later with the CIA. His group, which was also located in Oberursel, was in the process of compiling a detailed description of the workings of the Soviet Intelligence Operations and other specifications about the Red Army, material they had gathered during the war with the Soviet Union. It became my responsibility to translate that information.

Working hours at Oberursel were from nine to five on workdays and half a day on Saturday. I found my job so fascinating that I would often go to the office and work after dinner, and occasionally on weekends.

My secretary typed my handwritten translations. Several times a week I would confer with one of Mr. Singer's principal deputies, a former German teacher from Wisconsin, who reviewed my work. That was always a very stimulating occasion. My reviewer, a native-born American, had an excellent command of German but was not familiar with the nuances of "Nazi-Deutsch" (the way the German language had been used, or better said misused, under the Nazis). Therefore, we had many long discussions regarding the meaning of certain words or phrases. Moreover, often we would also discuss politics and other topics outside the assignment. He also improved my English phrasing. As I finished each chapter, it was transmitted to Washington. Heaven knows whatever became of this work. (In 1956 Major General Reinhard Gehlen, the German officer whose work I had translated, became the first head of West Germany's Federal Intelligence Service—*Bundes-Nachrichtendienst*, the German equivalent of the CIA.)

On some occasions, I also participated in interrogating new prisoners, usually border crossers, i.e. mostly men who had been arrested trying to cross illegally from the Soviet Zone of Occupation to the American side.

As my enlistment was ending, Mr. Singer asked me to stay on as a civilian employee but I declined. I felt that it was more important to my future that I go to college, in spite of the "princely" salary he offered of $100 weekly with free board. (That offer was higher than the starting salary I received three years later after having graduated from college.) I also longed to be able to live in the U.S., the country of which I had become a citizen but hardly knew. Therefore, Army service completed, I prepared to return to the States.

Life had been good in occupied Germany. Eastern European men staffed the camp at Oberursel. The Germans had deported these men during the war from their homes in Poland and Hungary, but they had refused repatriation after the war. The food was well-prepared by them, with fresh Danish milk and butter on a daily basis and excellent steaks at least once a week. (Please note that I am talking only about the enlisted men's mess hall.) Our rooms, formerly German officers' barracks, two enlisted men per room, were also taken care of by the "foreigners" and a few former German soldiers. Even our rifles were cleaned by them—but under supervision. The only Army disciplines I remember were the requirement for mandatory calisthenics every workday morning at 7:00, as well as occasional participation in parades.

Frankfurt was about a 20-minute streetcar ride away. The Army also had arranged for a special taxi service that for literally a few pennies transported us between the city and camp. Apart from my short trip to Berlin, which I have discussed in another chapter, I took some excursions to Bavaria, Luxembourg and Strasbourg, all areas that I had never before visited.

Despite all these perquisites, my entire stay in Germany had difficulties not easily explainable. I found it strange to get along with Germans, in spite of the fact that they were extremely polite and deferential. I was young and inexperienced and had not forgotten that I had been forced from my home by a criminal regime of the country that, now that the war was over and the "Cold War" had begun, had suddenly become "our friend." In addition, as my description about my work showed, we were now actually collaborating with our former enemies—who only a few years earlier would have killed me as they did members of my family.

The result was that I could not and would never

discuss the Nazi past with any German. If on occasion that subject came up, I would usually hear my German partner telling me that he or she never knew of the atrocities that had happened. I never challenged anyone. I also never admitted that I had been born and lived in Germany or that I was Jewish. In preparation, as part of my naturalization, I had changed my last name from Burstein to Burton. My certificate of naturalization, dated March 5, 1946 carries a note on the back (at my request) which reads: "Name changed by decree of Court from Bernhard Burstein as a Part of the Naturalization on March 5, 1946. C. W. Broadfoot, Clerk Superior Court, by (signed) W. N. Tillinghast, Deputy Clerk Superior Court." My parents never changed their name to Burton, and my father was actually annoyed at me for doing so. However, I knew I was eventually going to be sent to the American occupation Army in Germany. Burstein is a German-sounding name, and I did not want my origins to be known.[83]

We are talking about the years 1947/1948. At that time, English was not as commonly known as it is now.

---

[83] I have never seriously investigated the origin of the name Burstein. I believe that it is probably the German spelling of a Russian village name. Yet, I remember a bizarre, different explanation. In the spring of 1933— while I still attended an elementary school—the teacher, already at that early point a card-carrying member of the Nazi party (and hence a "Nazi by conviction," as I have explained in the chapter "Meeting Otto"), "explained" the background of all the names of the pupils in the class. He correctly mentioned that names like Bäcker, Müller and Wagner ("baker," "miller" and "coach-builder" in English) represented certain professions. Then he came to my name and theorized that the first syllable BUR was probably a derivation of the word *bauer* (farmer) and that my forefathers had worked on the land. Though he did not say so explicitly, this explanation tied in with the Nazi ideology that all Germans were hard-working people who derived their livelihoods from honorable professions. This teacher was always very nice to me. It was generally known that I was Jewish. However, at no time did he make any anti-Semitic remarks in my presence, and he "described" *all* names within the new framework, and did not mention that I was Jewish. However, even as a nine-year-old I did not buy his conclusion, but I was too smart (or too timid) to argue his point.

That meant that no German with whom I ever had any contact realized that I spoke English with a German accent. However, everyone marveled at the outstanding American school system that produced students like me who spoke such correct and accent-free German. Not once did I refute that observation either. Within the camp at Oberursel, I was the valued German translator; outside the camp, I became a German-speaking American phenomenon.

I acquired a circle of German "friends"—not just girlfriends, but through them also families who would invite me to some of their parties, a wedding and to other events. One family included the Chief of Police of Oberursel. When the latter had some problems with an overpopulation of small animals (and the farmers complained), I was able to get him involved with the chief of the guard battalion at the camp, which helped him to rid the area of the pests. This German Chief of Police became a "good" friend with whom I corresponded briefly even after my return to the States.

In retrospect, I realize that I made many mistakes in these relationships. With 20/20 hindsight and greater life experience I now feel that I should have challenged my German "friends." I could have talked about religion, Auschwitz or even about my own short stay in the "transit camp." I could have mentioned that relatives and dear friends were killed by a German criminal regime. However, I did not do so. It was not difficult to believe their claims that they were not aware of the atrocities; as far as I remember Oberursel might not have had any Jews before the onset of the Hitler regime (or they had left shortly thereafter). Furthermore, when my parents and I left Germany in July 1941 we were aware only of "work camps" that had been established for German Jews in occupied Poland. But we were unaware of extermination camps or of the ghettos that had been created even earlier. Therefore it is likely true that the Germans in Oberursel were not aware of the full extent of the "final solution" until after the war—and yet I still feel now that I should have challenged their statements.

Yet, when you review Holocaust literature you will find that in 1947/48 and even later, people did not discuss their pasts. That only occurred after many more years. So I was not the exception at that time. And still it was a mistake.

On April 8, 1948, I was discharged from the Army. That same day I returned to my parents' apartment in Guttenberg, NJ. Within days, I started my quest to enter a college in the fall. I had no conception of what that meant except for the strong belief that to advance in life in my new homeland I would need higher education. At that moment, I did not even know what I should study. Three years later, I had obtained my BS in Business Administration, with honors, from Rutgers University. In June 1954 I received an MBA from NYU, and in September 1955 I became a Certified Public Accountant. I was the first member of my family ever to have accomplished a college education.

I could have been discharged from the Army somewhat earlier, but I extended my service voluntarily. The main reason was the fact that I had realized early on the precarious financial situation of my parents and myself. A college education costs money. Yet, with my Army service I was able to take advantage of one of the greatest U.S. benefits ever enacted—the "GI Bill of Rights." My total service time was 28 months. The government in turn paid for my three years as an undergraduate student and about one half of the expenses towards my MBA. Additionally, while studying full-time, I received a stipend for living expenses of $75 monthly while I was single and $125 as a married man.

*Aboard Hitler's
"Stadt Köln"
Ha, ha, ha.*

August 1947

The U.S. Navy had captured Hitler's yacht *Stadt Köln* (City of Cologne) in 1945. During the early post-war years she became an occasional excursion boat for GIs. This picture shows me on a Rhine cruise aboard the yacht in August 1947. At the bottom are the comments I wrote on the back.

18

Helga

UPON MY RETURN from Army service, I reestablished contact with some of the few friends I knew from Germany and Cuba who now lived in the New York metropolitan area. Thus I met Robert Ronald again, my good friend and classmate from Havana who had left Cuba about a year after I did. In our first telephone conversation in April 1948, he asked me what I was going to do on the forthcoming Memorial Day weekend. He also mentioned that he had become a member of a German-Jewish ski club, which would hold its final get-together for the 1947–1948 season at Lake Hopatcong, NJ. Since I had no other plans, I readily accepted his invitation to spend a few days with him and his friends. I am not a skier but this was an "après-ski meeting."

The morning after my arrival at Lake Hopatcong Robert was busy playing tennis. Therefore, he asked me to accompany another member of the club to the railroad station to pick up a latecomer. That latecomer was a young woman by the name of Rose-Marie Helga Riemer (everyone at the club called her Rose-Marie). By the end of the long weekend, I had fallen in love with her. Within five weeks, on July 4, we decided to get married, and the ceremony took place about a year later on June 5, 1949. In spite of these quick decisions, we were happily married until Helga's death on September 14, 2004.

Helga had survived the entire Nazi period in Germany and arrived in the U.S. by herself, a "victim of Nazism," on March 14, 1947. (By coincidence that was the same day that I graduated from the CIC school in Baltimore.) With the help of some distant relatives, she had found a job as a bookkeeper and secretary in the diamond industry and had started to attend Hunter College at night.

While we were dating and even many years into our marriage, we did not talk about the horrible problems she had overcome in Germany: the accidental death of her non-Jewish father, her confinement in a Gestapo jail and the murder of her mother in Auschwitz. I shall discuss these tragic points in detail later in this chapter.

On May 8, 1945, the day Nazi Germany surrendered, Helga had found herself in Munich, staying at her sister's apartment. That same day (and not quite 20 years old), she was engaged to work as the first German interpreter for the U.S. Military Government in Bavaria. A letter of recommendation from her supervisor is printed at the end of this chapter.

At the urging of our children, Helga started, around 1980, to write about her own experiences. Unfortunately, she never completed her remembrances. It might have been too hard for her. However, following these explanations is her short unfinished manuscript. I have added footnotes to her writing where I believed additional information to be helpful. Yet, with the exception of the addition of the English translation of a German poem she had quoted, I have left her comments substantially unedited.

Helga's Unfinished Letter to Vivian, Monica And Mimi

Dearest ...

I am not sure that one ought to revive the past. There are times when it is better to forget it or to bury it because there is nothing you can do to change it. Besides, it is painful. But you have asked me so often and so insistently—you have even bought me a tape recorder to make it easier—that I have decided to tell you as much as I can remember about Germany, the Nazis and what it was like to live in Nazi Germany then.

It is ancient history now and more than 30 years have passed since it happened. There are many things that I have forgotten and some things I do not want to remember. Yet, it is probably good to talk about it, to gain distance and become less tied to it. I feel like Kafka bearing his soul. However, I am not Kafka and do not write on the Eve of Atonement.

Let me tell you something about my background. I was born in Saarbrücken, the "coal pot" of Germany, a stone's throw from France. Saarbrücken was and still is an industrial city; it is neither as beautiful as Munich nor does it have the culture of Berlin or the liveliness of Cologne. In my time, Saarbrücken was a city like many others in Germany with its share of culture and mediocrity. I grew up in the city.

Our apartment house faced the Ludwigskirche[84] and a large square where I used to play with my friends. My family was not wealthy but we lived well. My father taught Greek and Latin at the Gymnasium and somehow

---

[84] Ludwig's Church (completed in 1775) is considered one of the three most beautiful Protestant Baroque churches in Germany. The church, destroyed during WWII, has been rebuilt.

most people knew him. I do not know whether my parents had a "good" marriage. They probably did but the strain and stress of the time, living under Hitler, took its toll. Despite occasional unpleasant quarrels, they were much devoted to each other and to their children. It did not help much. They could not prevent what they tried so desperately to prevent. In the end, we were all torn apart anyway.

I grew up like everybody else in the neighborhood with friends, playmates and a school to walk to. Nothing special! My family seemed to be like everyone else's and neither my sister nor I knew that something was wrong. My parents did not believe in airing troubles in front of their children so we remained in a state of "blessed" ignorance. Sometimes I heard them discuss politics, mentioning Hitler's name, but overall Germany's "Führer" and his cronies were remote to me at that time. In 1933, he played no role in my childhood yet. Saarbrücken, or rather the Saarland of which Saarbrücken was the capital, led a separate existence then. It was not part of Germany but functioned since the end of WWI under French supervision, mandated by the League of Nations. In 1935, after Hitler had been in power for two years the Saarland was to vote for or against return to Germany. It voted overwhelmingly in favor of return.[85] *Heim ins Reich* was the slogan and "heim" (home) they went.

I became aware of some difficulties for the first time (in 1935) when I was less than ten years old. I can still see myself leaning against the bathtub watching my father shave. It was a Sunday morning; I had risen up early, waiting for my parents to get up.

It had been on my mind for a long time and now I

---

[85] A plebiscite was held in the territory on January 13, 1935, supervised by the League of Nations. 90.3% of those who voted were in favor of joining Germany.

wanted to ask the question. However, I was scared or perhaps it was more a sense of unease that I felt. I knew I had to ask the question and finally I blurted it out. "Can I be a member of the Hitler Youth?" I do not remember my father's anger; he probably said "no."[86] However, I do remember my mother coming in later. I could tell she was upset. Her face was white and drawn. She said she would give me a fountain pen (an unheard of gift in those days) if I did not ask again to join. There was an expression on my mother's face which I had never seen before. It was as if fear had taken over her face. She did not explain anything but I knew I would never ask again. Not because I had taken the pen that I did not want, or because I felt I had made a deal, but because I sensed something was wrong and the wrongness was terrible. It was as if a feeling of terror had invaded her, and through her, it entered me.

You are probably gasping: how could I, a half-Jewish child, have wanted to join the Hitler Youth? But remember, I did not know I was half Jewish. I knew only how I felt to be the only child in class who stood alone when the teacher asked "Who is *not* a member of the Hitler Youth?" It is hard to face a wall of silent children and see them stare week after week when the same question is repeated. I wanted to be part of the crowd, to be like all others. Instead, I stood out. I was an outsider of society at an early age.

My parents wanted to protect us from the harsh reality of being second-rate human beings. Perhaps they thought there was enough time to tell us later when we were older, understood more and could absorb the shock that Hitler was embarking on a program to get rid of the Jews. Perhaps they thought that nothing much would

---

[86] Helga would not have been permitted to join the Hitler Youth even if her parents had wanted her to, as membership was closed to those who had two Jewish grandparents.

happen to the Saarland, the region that led a separate existence, so to speak, from the end of World War I until 1935 when she voted to be reunited with Germany.

We simply did not know that my mother was Jewish. Neither of my parents went to church and my father was fond of saying that "religion is the opiate of the poor." He despised organized, dogmatic religion. My sister and I did not pick up the clues that must have been there until much later. How can you blame parents for wanting to give their children a happy, carefree childhood? Can you blame them for not preparing their children for what was in store for them?

When at last I did find out, the knowledge hit me like a ton of bricks. It was shortly after the death of my father, when I came upon a letter which my uncle had written to my father. He was my father's youngest brother Hans (17 years his junior), an avowed Nazi who was later killed in the war. He advised my father to get a divorce because my mother was a "non-Aryan." It would make things easier for him professionally, he pointed out, and my sister and I would be assured a normal childhood, since it was only fair that my father would take the children away from the Jewess. Thus the reasoning of a Nazi and "well-meaning" relative.

Hitler came to power in 1933. In 1935 the so-called Nürnberg Laws disenfranchised the Jews and prohibited marriages between "Aryans" (as Hitler called his pure-blooded Germans) and non-Aryans or other undesirables (like Jews or gypsies, for example) in order to preserve the "purity" of the German blood, which Hitler considered the basis for the continued existence of the German people. In 1941, the Jews were forced to wear in public the yellow Star of David, which bore the inscription *Jude* (Jew) and was worn visibly on the left side of their clothes. From 1933 on Jews were pushed out of their jobs. Non-Jews married to

Jews could not hold civil service jobs.

My father was a civil servant (teachers are civil servants in Germany) who was kicked out in 1937. For him teaching had been his whole existence. He loved it and he was good at it. He fought his expulsion as long as he could, tried unsuccessfully to become the principal of a private school, and when he failed, he attempted to get a visa to Chile. However, the private school would not accept him because he was "tainted" with a Jewish wife, and Chile did not take him because he had no sponsor, no job waiting and no money with which to ensure one or the other.

Therefore, it was decided that we were to leave Saarbrücken and move to Garmisch-Partenkirchen, a fairy-tale winter resort in the Bavarian Alps.[87] My parents liked the mountains and the clean air would help my father cope with his asthma. My sister and I would transfer to a local high school and eventually we would move to Munich.

That was the plan, the dream and the fantasy. The reality was different. My father died barely a year after we moved. He had been able to do some tutoring, thus supplementing his income; he did some mountain climbing and life seemed good to us in the remote mountain village.

Except that I hated school.

Other than that, I adjusted well enough to the new and different life. Then my father died. He was not killed by the Nazis; he did not commit suicide, he was not sick. He died from a poorly-tended multiple fracture of his leg, a fracture that he sustained in a sledding accident. One of his students had taken him down a steep hill on his sled and my father, in trying to slow down the racing sled, broke his leg. In a village in which broken legs were a daily occurrence during the winter months, my father's accident

---

[87] The site of the Winter Olympic Games in 1936.

was nothing to get excited about. Nevertheless, he died from it because the surgeon refused to check out the pain of which he was complaining for weeks. When my mother who was worried took him out of the hospital over the objections of the doctor and brought him to the university hospital in Munich, it was too late. Gangrene had set in and even amputation of the leg did not help anymore. After three operations, he was too weak to go on fighting for his life.[88]

For my mother his death quite literally became the beginning of the end. Things were bad for the Jews in 1938. It was the time of the *Kristallnacht* when synagogues were burned, thousands of Jewish stores were destroyed and Jewish men were rounded up and sent to concentration camps. As long as my mother remained married to a non-Jew, she was accorded some measure of protection. Now that he was dead, she could not count on anything. It was only a matter of time before she would be arrested.

Why then, if she knew she was in danger, did she not simply pack up and leave? The answer is that for someone without money there were no easy solutions, and no welcome mat was out to receive her. The British had set quotas which limited the flow of refugees into what was then Palestine; Switzerland did not take anyone without proof of sufficient funds for support, and America had its own set of immigration laws. The doors were closed for many Jews who did not have either connections or money. My mother had neither. Therefore, she stayed; she was trapped.

She did not realize that to remain in Garmisch-Partenkirchen was tantamount to committing suicide. In a small town, everyone is involved with his neighbor and

---

[88] Otto Riemer died on March 5, 1939.

knows more about him than he himself. Garmisch was no exception. What else did people who lived there all year have to do but gossip? My mother was the "town Jew," the curiosity, the outsider of society. Only one other woman was also Jewish and that was the daughter-in-law of Richard Strauss, the famous composer. She had been declared an *Ehrenarierin* (an honorary Aryan) by Hitler or one of his cronies in accordance with Göring's pronouncement *Wer Jude ist, bestimme ich* (I decide who is a Jew). There were rumors that Strauss had threatened to leave Germany if anyone touched his son's wife. Perhaps it was felt in Nazi circles that Germany could ill afford to lose its best artistic talents. Perhaps Hitler personally interfered. Be that as it may, Strauss's daughter-in-law seems to have been safe.[89]

Not so my mother. Periodically she would have to disappear, as she had done in the past, in order to avoid being arrested. She would go away for a few days, or a week, generally to a larger city such as Innsbruck or Munich, where she could be undetected, an anonymous person among anonymous people. She always lived in the shadow of disaster, never knowing when it would finally strike. There were curfews for her, arrests and near-arrests and her refusal to wear the Star of David. She never did. Eventually she was arrested and taken to a jail in Frankfurt.[90]

Frankfurt is an ancient city where trade and humanism lived side by side; a modern city known for its hustle and bustle, a metropolis throbbing with life. The twentieth century converted it into a city of death.

---

[89] She indeed survived the period unharmed.

[90] Helga's mother wrote her a pitiful letter from jail asking for her help. Upon reading it, Helga decided to leave Essen (where she temporarily lived with her aunt and uncle) and travel to Frankfurt to visit her mother.

I arrived in Frankfurt on an express train from Essen, a small suitcase in my hand, looking for the Hotel Frankfurter Hof and trying to look grown up. The day was Tuesday, the month November.[91] It was cold and wintry but otherwise not altogether unpleasant.

I was bewildered, scared and apprehensive, totally unsure of myself and equally uncertain of how to proceed. Yet, there was a distinct feeling of relief: I was doing something. I had come to see my mother and I was determined to accomplish this, no matter what the obstacles were.

My mother was in jail. In the clutches of Germany's most feared "Jew-hater" Heinrich Baab (who was subsequently brought to trial, convicted and sentenced to 250 years of hard labor).[92] She had been held in Frankfurt's infamous Gestapo headquarters and then sent to jail. I went the same way.

I had come to find my mother, to speak with her, to reassure her through my presence that my sister Gisela and I were alive. There was no lawyer who acted for me, no relative to advise me, no friend to accompany me. The circumstances did not allow the luxury of help and comfort. My aunt and uncle felt it unwise to come with me for fear of exposing my aunt's "Jewishness."[93] My non-Jewish relatives looked away. And so I was alone and on my own in an unfamiliar city, armed with a letter from my mother that she had written in jail. It was a pathetic letter,

---

[91] The year was 1942.

[92] *The New York Times* reported on April 5, 1950 that Heinrich Baab, a former Gestapo official, was sentenced to life imprisonment. His crimes, among others, consisted of arrest, mishandling and transport to Auschwitz and other concentration camps of Jewish partners in mixed marriages.

[93] While Helga used the word "unwise," it is my opinion that it was, unfortunately, the only possible reaction at that time. If her (Jewish) aunt—even accompanied by her non-Jewish husband—had tried to help, the result may well have been the aunt's arrest or worse.

a document of love and fear that had been censored and burnt in places. It was only partially legible.[94]

Therefore, I sought out the Gestapo to receive permission to see my mother wherever she was. And I walked into the lion's den.

The Gestapo headquarters was a huge, massive building, identified through a shiny brass plate and surrounded by a black cast iron fence. One enters it by ringing an ordinary doorbell, which is answered from within by pressing a button, and the door opens silently. A very simple and direct procedure to swallow its victims.

Three marble steps lead to a small window such as might be found in the offices of a diamond dealer on New York's 47th street. But the window at the Gestapo is not bullet-proof, as it would be in the diamond office. It need not be, because behind the glass sit those in power, the ones who rule over "life and death," the masters, Hitler's slaves, his supermen.

Bullets do not enter the building. Only frightened people do who diminish in size and shrink in fear.

Young people possess something that grownups have lost in the process of maturation: a blissful ignorance of the consequences of their actions. At times, it is taken for courage.

I was neither courageous nor unduly frightened when I approached the window. It was more a general nervousness that had taken hold of me. I did not know how to carry myself, how to phrase my question. I simply blurted out: "I came to see my mother Annie Riemer. Can you tell me where she is and what do I have to do to see her?"

The woman at the window asked for the name of my mother, date and place of birth, details of her arrest

---

[94] I have donated the original letter to the Jewish Museum in Berlin.

and motioned me to wait. She was neither friendly nor unfriendly, just coldly efficient.

Again, I was less afraid than on my guard. What if they kept me at headquarters, if I could not leave through the silent doors through which I came voluntarily? How would I get out? And I thought of looking for a bathroom. There was one on the first floor. Its windows were high and barred by iron gates.

The interrogation began three hours later. I was led into a large room. There was a table in the middle. Two people were pacing the floor and someone coolly told me he was "happy" to see me. They had waited for me knowing that I would come and they would personally see to it that I was sent to a KZ (concentration camp). After that, questions were fired at me. Where had my mother been hiding? Who had helped her? Who had informed her in Garmisch and who had sheltered her subsequently on her flight? And "how could this pig of a man, 'my father,' have married a Jewess?"

Something snapped inside me at this point. I was not scared and I did not care; I simply screamed at the Gestapo man who was Baab, infamous chief and henchman of the Frankfurt Gestapo: "How dare you insult my father? You are not fit to tie his shoelaces."

I draw a blank when I think of the rest of the interrogation. I remember the room, the lights, the Gestapo men but nothing else.

The next thing I remember is being shoved into a police van to be transported to prison (Frankfurt's infamous Gestapo jail).

And so I arrived at jail, a young girl clad in a powder blue wool dress with three buttons down the front and a narrow belt. It was the first dress I had ever sewn myself and I had worn it to show my mother that I could do things to make her happy, if only for a moment. She never saw the dress.

German jails are far from being pleasant. Attica is heaven by comparison to the German counterpart. In Frankfurt, there were no radios, no TVs, no books, no daily baths or showers.

There were also no rights.

From the beginning, I was placed in solitary confinement. I, a dangerous criminal of barely 17. If there is a hell somewhere after death, one of its components must surely be solitary confinement. It *is* hell!

You are alone with your thoughts for 24 hours a day. You cannot sleep; you cannot eat; you cannot see the sun. It is a naked stone cell with a cot and a blanket, a pail in the corner, a light bulb on the ceiling and a window too high to be reached. I tried, God knows. You are plagued by fear and doubts. You learn the meaning of despair and you understand why people succumb to brainwashing. You learn how torture works because you yourself are tortured. Isolation is a form of torture.

Bread brings back the memory of jail, black bread, hard crust, a thick crust of it. That and a poem by Goethe (Germany's greatest poet) which some prisoner, some tortured being, had scratched into the wood of a bleak jail. I carry this poem with me since then:

> *Wer nie sein Brot mit Tränen ass,*
> *Wer nie die kummervollen Nächte*
> *Auf seinem Bette weinend sass,*
> *Der kennt euch nicht, ihr himmlichen Mächte.*
> *Ihr führt ins Leben uns hinein,*
> *Ihr lasst den Armen schulding werden,*
> *Dann überlasst ihr ihn der Pein:*
> *Denn alle Schuld rächt sich auf Erden.*

(He who never ate his bread with tears, he who never, through miserable nights, sat weeping on his bed—he does not know you, Heavenly Powers. You lead us into life, you let the wretched feel guilt, and then you leave him to his pain—for all guilt avenges itself on earth.)[95]

Nothing is worse than total lack of communication to drive a person insane; one need only to find a method of absolute isolation. Sometimes I felt I was going insane. There was no contact with the outside and no information reached the inside. There was no hearing, no case, no lawyer, nothing but silence. People choose their own ways to remain in a situation such as this. Mine was to recite poetry silently. I had always liked ballads. Their rhyme, their melody intrigued me as a child and when my sister learned her first ballads for school, I learned them with her. They certainly came in handy. I thought of ways to contact my mother, of escaping. But those were the fanciful parts of my thinking. They did not cover adequately all my spare time. The rest was fear.

I did not go on a hunger strike. It was not necessary. I just could not eat. I drank the water and occasionally I ate a little bit of the black bread. However, whatever else there was, I left untouched. It was not a conscious course of action that I devised, but it did have results. After ten days of refusing to eat, I was transferred to a cell with other people.

Thus Ended Helga's Unfinished Letter

When Helga's aunt and uncle had not heard from her for more than a week after she had left their house in

---

[95] Translation copyright by Emily Ezust, from the *Lied and Art Song Texts*. The poem itself was written by Johann Wolfgang von Goethe in his novel *Wilhelm Meisters Lehrjahre* (Wilhelm Meister's Apprenticeship) in 1795/96.

Essen and were unable to reach her, they became extremely anxious. They contacted a lawyer in Frankfurt and requested his assistance. Fortunately, the lawyer was able to negotiate Helga's release several weeks later, most probably with bribes. However, any attempts to obtain her mother's release from jail proved useless. Anna Riemer was deported to Auschwitz, where she died on February 23, 1943, probably in the gas chamber.

The manner in which the date of my mother-in-law's death was confirmed seems almost unbelievable. In order for Helga to be declared a *Vollwaise* (orphan) and receive a pension from the government, written proof of her mother's death was required by the German authorities. Whoever applied for Helga's claim to an orphan's pension sought appropriate documentation. Under date of April 28, 1943 an official death certificate, or *Sterbeurkunde*, was issued stating that Anna Sara Riemer had died at 9:45 AM on February 23, 1943. The death certificate is pictured on page 176. Until I met Helga, I had never heard of such a certificate being issued.

Recently, my family received further verification of the date and time of Helga's mother's death. When the Soviet Army liberated Auschwitz in 1945, they took control of thousands of official documents, which they kept secret until 1989. Among the many archives that became public at that time were the so-called *Sterbebücher*, or "Death Books." These consist of 46 volumes of official records of the deaths of nearly 69,000 "registered" prisoners who died at the Auschwitz concentration camp between July 27, 1941 and December 31, 1943. (Any other such records kept by the Nazis were destroyed by them as the Soviet Army approached the camp.) Anna Riemer's name appears among the still-extant volumes. When my granddaughter Nicole visited Auschwitz in the summer of 2007 as part of a "Philosophy of Freedom" course, she made a request at the

Auschwitz Museum to receive copies of any information associated with her great-grandmother. A few weeks later, a page from a *Sterbebuch* arrived in the mail, containing the internal Nazi record of my mother-in-law's death. The record appears on page 174.

Living partially with her relatives in Essen, with her sister Gisela in Munich and during the school years in a private boarding school in Leipzig, Helga survived the remainder of the war years in Germany. The school specialized in language training. The wife of the school's owner/director was a native of Iceland, married to a German. The couple was aware of the fact that Helga was not "Aryan." Yet, they were instrumental in keeping Helga and a few other young women safely in their school. (Nazi laws prohibited the education of Jews.) The money from her orphan's pension helped her to pay for her attendance at school. Some two years later, toward the end of the war, Helga had become an exceptionally well-trained interpreter, fluent in English and Russian (including shorthand in these languages) and reasonably knowledgeable in French.

By the spring of 1945, Helga realized that the Soviet Army was on its way to occupy Leipzig. Therefore, she left the school and went to Munich to be with her sister and to await the arrival of the Western Allies. U.S. forces took Munich on April 30, 1945 and eight days later Helga started her work as interpreter for the Military Government.

Record of Anna Riemer's Death
from the Gestapo *Sterbebuch* (Death Record) at Auschwitz
Translation appears on following page

Nr. 10542/1943   (42)   C¹

Auschwitz, den _8. März_ 19_43_

D ie Anna Sara Riemer geborene Adler

evangelisch, früher mosaisch

wohnhaft Garmisch, Bayern

ist am 23. Februar 1943 _____ um _09_ Uhr _45_ Minuten

in Auschwitz, Kasernenstraße _____ verstorben.

D ie Verstorbene war geboren am _1.Dezember 1893_

in Krefeld

(Standesamt _____ Nr. _____)

Vater: Josef Adler, zuletzt wohnhaft in Dussendorf

Mutter: Henriette Adler geborene Birnzweig, zuletzt

wohnhaft in Dussendorf

D ie Verstorbene war — ~~nicht~~ ~~verheiratet~~ Witwe von Otto Riemer

Eingetragen auf ~~mündliche~~ — schriftliche Anzeige des Arztes Doktor der

Medizin Kitt in Auschwitz vom 23. Februar 1943

D — Anzeigende

~~Vorgelesen, genehmigt und~~ ~~unterschrieben.~~

Die Übereinstimmung mit dem
Erstbuch wird beglaubigt.

Auschwitz, den 8. 3. 1943

Der Standesbeamte
In Vertretung

Der Standesbeamte
In Vertretung
Quakernack

Todesursache: Herzmuskelinsuffizienz

Eheschliessung de Verstorbenen am _____ in _____

(Standesamt _____ Nr. _____).

174

No 10542/1943

Auschwitz, March 8, 1943

Anna Sara Riemer nee Adler, Protestant formerly Mosaic[96] resident of Garmisch, Bavaria died on February 23, 1943 at 9:45 AM at Kasernenstrasse, Auschwitz.[97]
The deceased was born on December 1, 1893 in Krefeld.
Father: Josef Adler, last residence Dusseldorf.
Mother: Henriette Adler nee Birnzweig, last residence in Dusseldorf.
The deceased was the widow of Otto Riemer.
Recorded upon written statement by Kitt, MD in Auschwitz on February 23, 1943.
Authenticated in accordance with the primary records.
Auschwitz, March 8 1943

Signed
Quakernack
Representative of Registrar

Cause of death: Heart muscle insufficiency[98]

---

[96] The word "Mosaic" (in German *mosaisch*), a derivative of "Moses," was used in German "officialese" to denote Jewish. Both records state that Anna Riemer was a convert to Protestantism. Although as Helga described, her father was not a religious man, nevertheless he asked that his wife convert to Christianity at the time of their marriage. Knowledge of her mother's conversion was a source of discomfort to Helga. She and I never speculated about the reason behind it, though it certainly was not religious. However, even at the time of her parents' marriage in 1922 there was latent anti-Semitism in Germany, particularly in the smaller towns. It is likely that Helga's father, especially as a government employee, was concerned about this, and that it played a part in his motivation.
[97] Both documents list "Auschwitz Kasernenstrasse," a relatively common street name, as the place of death. This was part of the effort by the Nazis to hide their crimes. They sought to create the impression that their victims had simply died on a given street in the city of Auschwitz in Nazi-occupied Poland.
[98] "Heart muscle insufficiency" is one of several causes of death routinely recorded in the *Sterbebücher* as another part of the Nazi cover-up. No Auschwitz inmate is stated in internal Nazi documentation to have died as a result of forced inhalation of Zyklon B gas.

Official *Sterbeurkunde* (Death Certificate)
for Anna Riemer
Translation appears on following page

Sterbeurkunde

(Standesamt II Auschwitz ——————————Nr. —————)

Die Anna Sara Riemer geborene Adler ————————————

————— ———————— evangelisch, früher mosaisch. —————

wohnhaft Garmisch, Bayern ———————————————

ist am— 23. Februar 1943 ————— um — 09 — Uhr — 45 — Minuten

in Auschwitz, Kasernenstraße ————————————— verstorben.

Die Verstorbene war geboren am 1. Dezember 1893 ——————

in Krefeld ————————————————————————

(Standesamt ————————————————— Nr. —————)

Vater: Josef Adler, zuletzt wohnhaft in Düsseldorf —————

Mutter: Henriette Adler geborene Birnzweig, zuletzt —————
wohnhaft in Düsseldorf —————————————————

Die Verstorbene war – nicht – verheiratet. Witwe von Otto Riemer

————————————————————————————
————————————————————————————

Auschwitz, den 28. April —————— 194 3

Der Standesbeamte
In Vertretung

Gebührenfrei

Certificate of Death

Registry Office II Auschwitz

Anna Sara Riemer nee Adler, Protestant formerly Mosaic resident of Garmisch, Bavaria died on February 23, 1943 at 9:45 AM at Kasernenstrasse, Auschwitz.

The deceased was born on December 1, 1893 in Krefeld.

Father: Josef Adler, last residence in Düsseldorf

Mother: Henriette Adler nee Birnzweig, last residence in Düsseldorf

The deceased was the widow of Otto Riemer.

Auschwitz, April 28, 1943
Signed [signature illegible]
Representative of Registrar

[Stamp:]
Registrar's Office II
Auschwitz—District of [illegible]

Free of charge

Recommendation from Helga's supervisor
(text also appears on page 192)

OFFICE OF MILITARY GOVERNMENT FOR BAVARIA
CIVILIAN PERSONNEL OFFICE
APO 170

Munich 24 August 1946.

SUBJECT: Letter of Recommendation

TO : Whom it may concern.

This is to certify that Miss Helga Riemer has been
employed with this Military Government since May 8th, 1945.
She was the first interpreter at the Office of Regional Military
Government for Land Bavaria to work with the Americans since
the occupation of Munich/Germany.

Miss Riemer has been doing an excellent job in her
capacity as an interpreter, translator, secretary and
receptionist. She interpreted and simultaneously took notes
in the most important conferences held between the competent
officers of the Civil Administration & Local Government Branch
of the Regional Military Government and the later appointed
German Ministerpraesident and his ministers. Her work
included translating of the German governmental plans and
assistance at the investigations of former German officials
of the Bavarian Government. She also verbally translated the
speeches of Ministerpraesident Schaeffer which later were
broadcast over the radio.

Her work as a secretary has also been done very efficiently
and skillfully. She set up the files for the office, took
care of the incoming and outgoing correspondence, and took
dictations in English shorthand.

Miss Riemer is leaving for the States with my best
wishes for the future.

Dr. Andrew Ganfmanas,
Chief, Civ. Pers. Office.

178

The Identification of Jews

In Helga's letter to her daughters, she had referred to the 1941 law requiring Jews to wear the "yellow Star of David." She also mentioned her mother's refusal to comply. This degrading law did not apply to my parents or to me since we had left Germany 47 days before its announcement.

Here is a picture of the required identification (actual size). Note the insulting spelling of the word *Jude* in make-believe Hebrew characters. The "Police Regulation Regarding the Identification of Jews" appears on the following pages, in English and in the original German.

Police Regulation Regarding the Identification of Jews
Order of September 1, 1941 (German Law Gazette I Page 547)

1) (1) Jews, as defined by the Nuremberg Law of November 14, 1935, who are above the age of six, are prohibited from appearing in public without a *Judenstern* (Jew Star).
(2) The *Judenstern* consists of a palm of the hand sized, black-bordered yellow, six-pointed star with black label *Jude* (Jew). The *Judenstern* is to be sewn visibly onto the left breast of the garment.

2) (a) Jews are prohibited to leave their residential area without carrying a written permission issued by the local police.
(b) Jews are also prohibited from wearing any decorations or insignias.

3) Paragraphs 1 and 2 are not applicable for
(a) the Jewish member of a mixed marriage with children who are not recognized as Jews even if the marriage does not exist anymore or if their only son had been killed during the present war.
(b) the Jewish member of a childless mixed marriage during the duration of the marriage.

4) (1) Whoever violates paragraphs one or two, whether deliberately or negligently, will be punished with a monetary fine up to 153 Reichsmark or imprisonment up to six weeks.
(2) Further police security measures as well as criminal procedures carrying a higher punishment remain unaffected.

5) (This paragraph states that this Police Regulation is also applicable to Bohemia and Moravia.)

6) The Police Order is effective 14 days after publication (September 19, 1941).

Notes about the translation:
1) Paragraph 2 b refers to German Jewish veterans of World War I who had received medals for their service in the Imperial German Army. These medals could no longer be worn.
2) Paragraph 4 (2) means in effect that Jews caught without a *Judenstern* could be incarcerated in a concentration camp.
3) Bohemia and Moravia were the names given to the former Czechoslovakia annexed by Germany in 1939.

Polizeiverordnung über die Kennzeichnung der Juden

Verordnung vom 1. Sep. 1941 (Reichsgesetzblatt I S. 547)

Auf Grund der Verordnung über die Polizeiverordnungen der Reichsminister vom 14. November 1938 (Reichsgesetzbl. I S. 1582) und der Verordnung über das Rechtsetzungsrecht im Protektorat Böhmen und Mähren vom 7.Juni 1939 (Reichsgesetzbl. I S. 1039) wird im Einvernehmen mit dem Reichsprotektor in Böhmen und Mähren verordnet:

§ 1
(1) Juden (§ 5 der Ersten Verordnung zum Reichsbürgergesetz vom 14. November 1935 - Reichsgesetzbl. I S. 1333), die das sechste Lebensjahr vollendet haben, ist es verboten, sich in der Öffentlichkeit ohne einen Judenstern zu zeigen.
(2) Der Judenstern besteht aus einem handtellergroßen, schwarz ausgezogenen Sechsstern aus gelbem Stoff mit der schwarzen Aufschrift "Jude". Er ist sichtbar auf der linken Brustseite des Kleidungsstücks fest aufgenäht zu tragen.

§ 2
Juden ist es verboten
a) den Bereich ihrer Wohngemeinde zu verlassen, ohne eine schriftliche Erlaubnis der Ortspolizeibehörde bei sich zu führen;

b) Orden, Ehrenzeichen und sonstige Abzeichen zu tragen.

§ 3
Die §§ 1 und 2 finden keine Anwendung
a) auf den in einer Mischehe lebenden jüdischen Ehegatten, sofern Abkömmlinge aus der Ehe vorhanden sind und diese nicht als Juden gelten, und zwar auch dann, wenn die Ehe nicht mehr besteht oder der einzige Sohn im gegenwärtigen Kriege gefallen ist;
b) auf die jüdische Ehefrau bei kinderloser Mischehe während der Dauer der Ehe.

§ 4
(1) Wer dem Verbot der §§ 1 und 2 vorsätzlich oder fahrlässig zuwiderhandelt, wird mit Geldstrafe bis zu 153 Reichsmark oder mit Haft bis zu sechs Wochen bestraft.
(2) Weitergehende polizeiliche Sicherungsmaßnahmen sowie Strafvorschriften, nach denen eine höhere Strafe verwirkt ist, bleiben unberührt.

§ 5
Die Polizeiverordnung gilt auch im Protektorat Böhmen und Mähren mit der Maßgabe, daß der Reichsprotektor in Böhmen und Mähren die Vorschrift des § 2 Buchst. a den örtlichen Verhältnissen im Protektorat Böhmen und Mähren anpassen kann.

§ 6
Die Polizeiverordnung tritt 14 Tage nach ihrer Verkündung in Kraft.

Thank You

AROUND 1994 I HAD decided to leave some notes to my grandchildren explaining how the years of the Nazi regime had influenced my life. Luckily, my parents and I had left Germany, albeit with little time to spare, and eventually landed in the U.S. The preceding pages are the compilation of these notes. I did not put them together all at once but in many bits over several years. Some years I might not have written more than a page or two and other years I became more productive.

I also spent many days at the library of the Leo Baeck Institute,[99] the New York Public Library and at other local libraries in Nassau County. My object was to become familiar with at least some of the many books and articles that have been published about the years I had chosen to discuss. While I did not study all anti-Jewish laws and regulations promulgated by Nazi Germany during the regime's more than 12 years in power, I daresay I at least perused them all. I do not regret the time spent. It was a laborious exercise but it helped me greatly to improve my understanding of that time's history.

These reminiscences are not necessarily exciting.

---

[99] This institution is a research center offering the most comprehensive documentation for the study of German Jewish history. It was named after Rabbi Leo Baeck (1875–1956), the leader of German Jewry until his own deportation to the Theresienstadt concentration camp in January 1943. Several foreign institutions had offered to help him escape Germany when that was still possible, but he refused to abandon his community. He lived and taught in Great Britain after his liberation.

However, here they are, and they should be of interest to my daughters and my grandchildren. I hope other readers may find them educational.

Janis Weissman, whom I married in October 2009, served as my first and most valuable editor of all of the raw material I had compiled. Her incisive questions and suggestions spurned me on to complete the task and I am most grateful to her.

My second cousin Linda Kibak helped me constantly with the technical aspect of writing on the computer, at the beginning an unfamiliar territory for me. She actually made the computer work for me. I thank you Linda!

I had also chosen to show specific pages or chapters to a number of other people including Phil Kibak, Trudy Gutman and Robert Ronald. All these relatives, friends and acquaintances have my deepest thanks for their valuable suggestions and in pointing me in the right direction.

I am deeply indebted to my editor Miriam Berger who undertook to review the entire book. Miriam's attention to detail, her sound judgment and her outstanding knowledge of the period encouraged me to rethink many aspects of my writing. Her assistance in finalizing these memoirs was invaluable.

Helga received her M.A. degree at New York University in 1967. The title of her master's thesis (written in German) was *Gebrauch und Bedeutung des Grotesken in Günter Grass' Novelle „Katz und Maus"* (Use and Meaning of the Grotesque in Günter Grass's Novella "Cat and Mouse"). She continued her education at NYU, completing the required courses for the PhD degree and passing the oral examination. Although she wrote some 80 pages of her dissertation, she never completed it. That work had been planned to explore "Women's Liberation in German Literature." Eventually Helga became an associate professor at Hofstra University, specializing in modern German literature, and taught at C. W. Post College.

I had started this book with the foreword from Erich Maria Remarque's novel *All Quiet on the Western Front*. Let me complete my writing by quoting one paragraph from Helga's master's thesis:

> *War die Zeit des ersten Weltkrieges schon sinnlos und absurd, so war die des zweiten Weltkrieges unvergleichlich sinnloser und grauenhafter. Der gesunde Menschen-verstand kann es kaum begreifen, dass die Ungeheuerlichkeiten der Hitlerzeit von einem so genannten zivilisierten Volk verbrochen wurden. ... Die Vergangenheit kann nicht einfach links liegen gelassen, der Wahnsinn einer Generation nicht zugedeckt werden. Dazu ist zuviel geschehen.*

The time of the First World War was already senseless and absurd; but the time of the Second World War was incomparably more senseless and more gruesome. Common sense can hardly comprehend that the atrocities of the Hitler regime were perpetrated by a so-called civilized nation. ... The past cannot simply be ignored; the madness of a whole generation cannot be covered up, for that too much had happened.

Letter from Henry Kamm

* * * * *

The New York Times
ROME BUREAU
CORSO VITTORIO EMANUELE 11, 154

TEL. 654-8293 – 659-889

September 11, 1984

Dear Mr. Burton,

Your letter to my editor stirred memories, still vaguely melancholic. The customs man who came to my house, a year later, allowed us to pack our books, each listed like yours, without Propaganda Ministry approval. But, because the war had progressed by 1941, our few belongings got no further than Switzerland. We could not afford their shipment to America. I wonder who's reading them now.

As I write this, I am once again surrounded by packers, the nth time. Tomorrow I shall be leaving for Greece.

Forgive this letter of reminiscence from a stranger, but yours stirred and brought back to the forefront of the mind images long forgotten.

Yours sincerely,

Henry Kamm

186

Letter from Dr. Lerner

* * * * * *

27 AV 5755
August 23, 1995

Mr. Bernard Burton
142 Monterey Drive
Manhasset Hills, NY 11040

Dear Mr. Burton,

I am moved beyond words by your letter to me and by the
copy of the letter to your grandchildren you so generously
shared with me.

Rabbi Jonas has been of interest to me for many years. As
one who has been deeply involved in opening the rabbinate
to women, I often wondered what became of her. Yours is
the only testimony I have from a person whose life she
touched. I would love to know what you thought at the
time. Was having a woman introduce herself that way not
perceived as strange?

The letter for your grandchildren was deeply moving,
particularly because it is so spare and factual. It is hard for
me to imagine, from the vantage point of the security of
Jewish life in late twentieth century New York, how one
came through these times. Was survival supported by the
ability to deal with the situation in optimistic fashion? The
miracle of you and your father finding yourselves just
outside the emigration ban is amazing.

I hope that you will choose to share your letter with some of the institutions which collect Holocaust memories. It is extremely moving.

May God grant you and yours a year of health, peace and fulfillment.

Sincerely,
Anne Lapidus Lerner
Dr. Anne Lapidus Lerner
Vice Chancellor

U.S. Army order for my first visit to Berlin after the end of World War II

* * * * * *

HEADQUARTERS
7707 EUROPEAN COMMAND INTELLIGENCE CENTER
APO 757 US ARMY
7 November 1947

SUBJECT: Leave Orders.

TO: T/5 Bernard H. Burton, RA42242306, 7707 ECIC, APO 757, US Army.

1. Under the provisions of Cir 57 EUCOM, dated 27 July 1947, Cir 9 EUCOM, dated 2 April 1947, as amended, and AR 600-115, the above named individual is hereby granted a leave of three (3) days, effective on or about 13 November 1947 for the purpose of visiting Berlin, Germany

2. The above named individual has sufficient funds to defray all anticipated expense incident to travel. No per diem nor reimbursement authorized for transportation ocsts (sic) advanced by this individual.

3. Travel by German aircraft is authorized on a space available basis. Facilities of ATC and EATS, such as messing, billeting and motor transportation will not be made available to this individual except at emergency stops due to weather or mechanical failure of the aircraft.

4. Class IV priority, as defined in Sec IV, Cir 83, Hq USFET, dated 5 June 1946, is authorized, but in no event will official duty personnel be displaced by this individual.

5. Outside the occupied zones, US Army messing, billeting and other facilities are not authorized and will not be provided and further, the bearer of this document will not request any commander to provide such.

6. Within the occupied zones, US Army messing, billeting and other facilities will be provided only after prior individual arrangements have been made and then only at the discretion of the commander concerned.

BY ORDER OF COLONEL THOROUGHMAN:

ROBERT A DORAN
1st Lt AGD
Adjutant

DISTRIBUTION
3-Individual concerned.
1-Headquarters Company
1-Adjutant (file)
1-Hq Comd

Time magazine article about the SS *Navemar*

* * * * * *

S.S. *NEVERMORE*

Scenes like this reunion were the bright side of the picture when the grimy Spanish freighter *Navemar* came to port in New York Harbor last week. Seven long weeks before, she had cleared from Seville, with a miserable human cargo, mostly war refugees. Built to accommodate 28 passengers, she had packed 1,120 aboard, into her hold and every usable part of the ship. Some of them had paid scalpers as much as $1,750 for their unforgettable passage.

According to their stories, they sickened on rotten food. In crude bunks they lay for days, some of them stricken with fever. Six died. Many slept in lifeboats (*left*) rather than endure the stinking hold. One physician said it was a "miracle" no epidemic broke out. They nicknamed their ship the *Nevermore*.

Recommendation from Helga's supervisor

* * * * * *

OFFICE OF MILITARY GOVERNMENT FOR BAVARIA
CIVILIAN PERSONNEL OFFICE
APO 170

Munich 24 August 1946.

SUBJECT: Letter of Recommendation
TO   : Whom it may concern.

This is to certify that Miss Helga Riemer has been
employed with this Military Government since May 8th,
1945. She was the first interpreter at the Office of Regional
Military Government for Land Bavaria to work with the
Americans since the occupation of Munich/Germany.
Miss Riemer has been doing an excellent job in her
capacity as an interpreter, translator, secretary and
receptionist. She interpreted and simoultaneously (*sic*)
took notes in the most important conferences held between
the competent officers of the Civil Administration & Local
Government Branch of the Regional Military Government
and the later appointed German Ministerpraesident and
his ministers. Her work included translating of the German
governmental plans and assistance at the investigations of
former German officials of the Bavarian Government. She
also verbally translated the speeches of Ministerpraesident
Schaeffer which later were broadcast over the radio.
Her work as a secretary has also been done very
efficiently and skillfully. She set up the files for the office,
took care of the incoming and outgoing correspondence,
and took dictations in English shorthand.
Miss Riemer is leaving for the States with my best
wishes for the future.

Dr. Andrew Ganfmanas,
Chief, Civ. Pers. Office.

CPSIA information can be obtained
at www.ICGtesting.com
Printed in the USA
LVOW08*0313180417
531175LV00017B/448/P

9 781105 871535